THE STORY OF THE BIBLE

THE STORY
OF THE BIBLE

How It Came to Us

Henry Wansbrough, OSB

Published in the United Kingdom by
Darton, Longman and Todd, Ltd.

Published in North America by
The Word Among Us Press
9639 Doctor Perry Road
Ijamsville, Maryland 21754
www.wordamongus.org

10 09 08 07 06   1 2 3 4 5

ISBN-13: 978–1–59325–072–0
ISBN-10: 1–59325–072–X

Cover design by John Hamilton and DesignWorks

Valentin de Boulogne (1594–1632)
Moses, c. 1620. Canvas, 131 x 103.5 cm.
Location: Kunsthistorisches Museum, Vienna, Austria
Photo Credit : Erich Lessing / Art Resource, NY

First page of the genealogy of Christ. From the Book of Kells, Irish
illuminated manuscript, ca. 800 CE.
Location: Trinity College, Dublin, Ireland
Photo Credit: Snark / Art Resource, NY

Made and printed in Great Britain

Library of Congress Cataloging-in-Publication Data

Wansbrough, Henry, 1934–
The story of the Bible : how it came to us / Henry Wansbrough.
p. cm.
Includes bibliographical references.
ISBN 1–59325–072–X (alk. paper)
1. Bible—Versions, Catholic—History.   2. Bible—History.   I. Title.
BS453.W36 2006
220.09—dc22
2005029716

CONTENTS

INTRODUCTION

In a recent seminar on the Bible which I was privileged to lead at
an American university even the most charming, responsive and
intelligent students began with the assumption that the printed
and embossed book they held in their hands somehow originated
in English. Perhaps God dictated the Old Testament to Moses,
much as Muslims believe that he dictated the Quran to
Mohammed. Then the evangelists added their bit, also in English,
and Paul his letters, written of course in English, to the various
communities he had founded.

Those students will not be unique in understanding the Bible
as a single book. In fact it often is a book, in that it is presented
within the covers of a single volume. However, it is really a collection of books, which do not seem to have been put within one set
of covers until some six or seven hundred years after Christ. They
are a disparate collection, including myth, folk-history, propa-
ganda, satire, laws, prayers, poetry, letters and fiction, united only
in one respect, namely that they all convey by one means or
another the ways of the God who was revealed to Abraham, and
whom Jesus called his Father. Some of them are no more than a
page or two, but were still treasured as transmitting something
valuable for Jews or Christians. These are not the only writings
which tell of the ways of God, nor the only works which set out to
tell of the life and teaching of Jesus and his appointed messengers.
They are the books which Christians accept as telling of the God
and Christ who form the centre of their quest and their life.

There are not many points on which all Christians agree, and
round the central core of these works accepted by all Christians
there is a penumbra of books which some Christians accept as
authoritative vehicles of the message of Christ while others do
not. But there is a remarkable degree of unanimity even on this,
and the number of disputed writings is few. Other books were
accepted in certain sections of the Church or for a certain
time and later fell away. In an era when books had to be copied
laboriously by hand they were just felt to be not worth the labour

of copying. Sometimes it was felt that the God or the Christ portrayed was not the God or the Christ whom Christians worship. Was the Christ whom Christians worship the sort of boy who would turn a man to stone simply for bumping into him? Was Peter given authority in the Christian community simply in order to bring a salted fish back to life? For centuries such writings disappeared until excavators in desert sands or forgotten libraries brought them to light again, at least in fragmentary form.

The books and booklets were written in three ancient languages of the Mediterranean world, Hebrew, Greek and Aramaic. To most of the Christian West these languages were almost unknown for a thousand years, at most the preserve of a tiny handful of scholars, while the language of law, diplomacy, courts and international communication was Latin. It was the language in which most written documents and almost all literature were couched until vernacular writings developed, well into the second millennium. As the vernacular languages developed they were for centuries felt to be unworthy vehicles of the Word of God. In addition, it was long felt by clergy and the noble literate classes alike that those who had insufficient learning to read and understand Latin could not be trusted to understand the complicated text of the Bible. Better that they should learn the stories as imparted to them by the clergy or depicted in the windows and on the walls of their churches. In England this feeling was reinforced by an unfortunate political accident: the unsuccessful Peasants' Revolt of 1382 twinned the right of every person to read the Bible with the right to other civil liberties. This set back translation into English by more than a century, leaving England lagging behind many continental countries.

This brings the story to the second half of the millennium, when certainly Greek and even Hebrew were becoming more widely known, at least among scholars. This gave the possibility, as the insistence of the sixteenth-century reformers on individual judgement gave the impetus, of translations from the original languages, cutting out the Latin version, which remained standard for the Roman Church. The stream here narrows somewhat, as we begin to concentrate on the great translations into English. Here I can only plead that English is the language in which this book will be published, and is also the language in which more people read the Bible than any other. There is further narrowing to come,

for the final theological chapter concentrates on the Roman
Catholic theology of the Second Vatican Council on the Bible.
Here again I plead that the insights formulated by Vatican II are
valuable to and widely accepted by Christians beyond the limits of
the Roman communion.

The purpose of this book, then, is to tell the story first of how
the Bible came to be formed, why some writings came to be
accepted as part of the Bible, while others were not. Then the
process by which it was translated into the Latin version and a
single book which was the standard text for a thousand years, a
process whose details still affect our Bibles today. Then the hard-
fought battle, involving kidnapping and murder, which forged the
incomparable monument of the first Bible in English, followed by
the more courtly political manoeuvrings which issued in the King
James Version, not neglecting other partisan translations on the
way. The final chapter is intended to show why it was all worth the
trouble.

Elements of this book have featured not only at the unnamed
American university, but at University College, London, and
Balamand University in the Lebanon. I am grateful to partici-
pants at all three universities for their insistence on clarity and
coherence. I am grateful also to Brendan Walsh of Darton,
Longman and Todd, a firm which has tolerated and encouraged
me for nearly 30 years, for his suggestion that I write the book.
Lastly I would like to thank Patrick Laver, who read the typescript
and picked up some of the more egregious errors.

ONE

How Did the Bible Come into Being?

The Old Testament

The Lindisfarne Gospels, a lavishly illustrated gospel-book probably penned in Lindisfarne about AD 800, has a marvellous illustration on the title-page of Matthew's gospel. Matthew is sitting, writing his gospel into a book. Just coming to meet him, with a finished gospel-book in his hand is God the Father, who at the same time draws back the curtain of revelation. Just for good measure, and to make doubly sure, hovering above Matthew's head is an angel with a long scroll, also contributing certainty to the gospel. Such was the ninth-century idea of inspiration and the production of the Bible. The reality is far less tidy.

The Jews divide the Hebrew Bible into three sections: the Law, the Prophets and the Writings. It would be neat to think of at least the first of these, the Law or the Pentateuch ('fivefold', meaning the first five books of the Bible: Genesis, Exodus, Leviticus, Numbers and Deuteronomy) as being written by Moses. Tradition holds that Moses is indeed the author of the Pentateuch, despite the fact that it narrates his death in the final chapter (Deuteronomy 34:5). This must be regarded as a myth, that is, a theological truth expressed in historical form, for the truth is far more complicated and far richer. Moses was indeed the 'author' in the sense that, by coaxing out of Egypt a rabble of fractious and depressed runaway slaves, and leading them to experience the meeting with God on Sinai which made them God's special people, he initiated or 'authored' the whole movement which led to the Pentateuch.

The Pentateuch

From a literary point of view, however, the Pentateuch has a fascinatingly diverse origin. Oral tradition was, of course, paramount, as the folk-stories of the wandering pastoral nomads, Abraham, Isaac and Jacob, were handed down from generation to generation by word of mouth for half a millennium with astonishing accuracy – but nevertheless as folk-history. One little couplet, the triumph Song of Miriam at the crossing of the sea (Exodus 15:21), could well go back word-for-word to the time of Moses, for poetry is remembered much longer than prose. There were stories of the great heroes of the people, and other stories explaining features of Hebrew custom or landscape, for every culture has such stories. Kipling's *Just So Stories* are favourite examples. A Shona story explains why the chicken scratches the ground! These were supplemented by a body of laws, outlining how it was necessary for these tribesmen and women to live as the People of YHWH. Again, the important myth of Moses' descent from the mountain, with the Ten Commandments inscribed on two tablets of stone, is an oversimplification. In the nineteenth century the discovery of the Code of the Mesopotamian legislator Hammurabi (1728–1686 BC) caused consternation among Christians, for this and other law-codes of the ancient Near East had laws largely similar to the Mosaic Code. Were they then not revealed to Moses by God? Even Cardinal Newman held that the Ten Commandments were inscribed on stone by the finger of God (does God have fingers?). Only in the sense that Moses and his successors, steeped in the laws and customs of the Near East, developed a case-law which laid down how people must live if they were to have God in their midst. They must protect the stranger and orphan as YHWH had protected them in Egypt. They must foster human dignity, allowing every person to stand tall before YHWH, dependent on no other lord. Such case-law continued to develop over centuries, revealing the successive living-conditions of Israel, first as pastoral nomads, then as agricultural farmers, finally as city-dwellers with king, temple and cult. The stories placed first in the Bible (Adam and Eve, Noah, the Tower of Babel) are among the latest to be composed. They show most clearly the preoccupations of a people living in exile in Babylon at grips with idolatry and other religions. They use the 'vocabulary' of the Babylonian myths to distinguish the exiles from their captors, to express their belief, not in a pantheon of quarrelling deities, but in a single, all-powerful God, who is hurt but never alienated by human failure and disobedience. Thus the Pentateuch grew and developed gradually, not reaching its final form until after the return from exile in Babylon.

The Prophets

The books of the great prophets, who attempted to shepherd Israel in God's ways, cannot be assumed to have been written from cover to cover like a modern book. The prophets were oral teachers, proclaiming the truth aloud by their words and often weird prophetic actions. Stories and sayings were subsequently gathered by disciples of these prophets, arranging them and linking them together by theme or subject-matter or merely link-words (Jeremiah 22 contains sayings about four successive kings over a period of more than 20 years; Ezekiel 21 contains five different prophecies linked by the word 'sword'). Around a nucleus of sayings and stories thus assembled were added – over decades or even centuries – other sayings, adaptations, liturgical doxologies, so that scholars are often at a loss to discern the kernel which goes back to the prophet under whose name the book stands. The same prophetic saying sometimes occurs in more than one book, and the variety within a single book makes it difficult to distinguish the core of the message. The sayings united in the book of Isaiah span at least two centuries, united by the awesome awareness of God as 'the Holy One of Israel', but those united under the name of Jeremiah are so diverse that he has been described as 'that Protean personality' (R.P. Carroll), with the implication that there is no single centre, no single common factor. Some scholars hold that this development of the prophetic literature spread over half a millennium, and that it was barely two hundred years before Christ that the prophetic corpus reached its final form and stopped growing.

The third component of the Hebrew Bible, 'the Writings', remained more flexible. It included such works as Proverbs, Ecclesiastes (Qoheleth) and the Song of Songs, as well as Psalms and the fascinating edifying stories of Esther and Ruth. It was not until nearly 200 years after Christ that decisions became firm within Judaism on which of these books 'soiled the hands'. (This expression was used because washing the hands before and after contact with the sacred books symbolised the transition from profane to sacred and from sacred to profane). The Dead Sea Scrolls suggest that other books, *The Book of Jubilees* and *First Henoch* were equally revered at Qumran as sacred writings. On the other hand, among the many thousands of fragments at Qumran, not one has been identified as containing any verses of Esther. Perhaps the sectaries at Qumran, rejecting the whole business of the Temple, disliked its focus on the Temple festival of Purim.

A Bible for Greek-speaking Jews and Christians

For Christians there is also a most important question concerning the value of the Greek Bible. In the Jewish colonies of the Diaspora, scattered over the trading cities of the eastern Mediterranean, there were many who no longer understood Hebrew. For them a Greek version of the Bible was produced. Legend, stemming from the *Letter of Aristeas* (310–311), has it that Ptolemy II in 275 BC ordered 72 scholars, working separately in 72 isolated rooms, to translate the Bible into Greek. At the end of 72 days they all emerged with an identical translation. Not surprisingly, the translation became known as the *Septuaginta* (Latin for 70, abbreviated LXX). The work of translation was in fact spread over two or three centuries, starting probably in Egypt in the third century and ending in the early first century before Christ. The importance of the legend is that it shows that the translation was regarded as authoritative and inspired. Besides the books translated from Hebrew, this Bible contained several books originally written in Greek. The importance of this translation is vast:

1. It became the Bible of the early Church. It is from this rather than from the Hebrew that the New Testament authors, writing, of course, in Greek, normally quote the scriptures.

2. We possess a full text of the LXX from the fourth century AD in the Codex Vaticanus, much of it in another fourth-century manuscript, the Codex Sinaiticus, and from the fifth century in the Codex Alexandrinus. Until the discovery of the Dead Sea Scrolls in 1946, these were half a millennium older than our oldest Hebrew witness to the biblical texts. At Qumran some quite extensive Hebrew Bible texts were discovered, including the whole Book of Isaiah. Apart from that, the earliest full copies of the Hebrew text are the Leningrad Codex of the tenth century and the partially complete Aleppo Codex of AD 925. Both of these important Hebrew texts belong to a single 'school' of manuscript tradition, stemming from the city of Tiberias on the shore of the Lake of Galilee,

so known as 'Tiberian'. The Greek text of the Bible provides access, therefore, to a version free of another five or six hundred years of copyists' mistakes. No matter how religiously careful – and there were dreadful threats against those who made mistakes – a copyist is, errors are bound to occur.

3. In certain cases a real advance in theology occurs in the LXX. The most famous case is Isaiah 7:14 where the original 'young woman' (not necessarily a virgin) is translated into Greek with the word 'virgin', a text used by Matthew 1:23 to confirm the virginal birth of Jesus: 'a virgin shall conceive and bear a son'. Another important theological advance is that there is also a whole series of passages where the hope of resurrection from the dead is far more robustly affirmed in the LXX than in the Hebrew. At Job 14:14 a tentative question in the Hebrew, 'Can the dead come back to life?' becomes a firm statement in the Greek, 'If a man dies, he shall live,' and similarly at Hosea 13:14.[1] It may be that the Greek, perhaps influenced by philosophy of the time, has been too positive in the translation, or that the Hebrew text which the Greek translator had before him was different from the Hebrew text we now possess, and that the Hebrew we now possess is less positive than the text seen by the Greek translator a thousand years earlier. In the intervening centuries the question could have been introduced into the Hebrew text by copyists.

There are plenty of other examples of differences and patterns of difference between the Hebrew text and the Septuagint, despite the care taken by the translators to keep close to the Hebrew text. Indeed, Hebrew word-forms and constructions are retained to the extent that the language is obviously translation-Greek, revealing the Hebrew thought and words beneath the Greek. One example of this is the retention of the infinitive for emphasis: the Hebrew expression clumsily translated 'listening you shall listen' really means 'you shall listen attentively'. The repeated word is used, for example, in Exodus 15:26. This very common Hebrew form often penetrates into English translations. It is hard to say which is the authentic Bible. Has the Greek progressed from the Hebrew or does it represent an older version?

Which, in either case, is to be regarded as the Word of God? Should it be the older version (whichever that may be), or the version which was used by the early Greek-speaking Christian writers?

A further difficulty is that the extent of the LXX, and so of the canon accepted at Alexandria, is unclear: different great manuscripts of the LXX have different books. Thus the oldest complete manuscript, the mid-fourth-century Codex Vaticanus, altogether omits the Books of Maccabees, while the fifth-century Codex Alexandrinus has four Books of Maccabees and fourth-century Codex Sinaiticus includes 1 and 4 Maccabees. To this day the standard edition of the LXX by Alfred Rahlfs (Stuttgart, Priviligierte Württembergische Bibelanstalt) prints 151 Psalms.

The New Testament

'Here! Read this!' It is natural and easy to imagine Peter at Pentecost distributing a boxful of copies of the New Testament to his listeners, or at least copies of the gospels. That would explain his message! Perhaps Paul would enclose a few copies of the gospels with his letters to the Thessalonians or the Romans. This would explain why he so seldom mentions the words and miracles of Jesus. But is the genesis of the New Testament any simpler than that of the Old?

Of course, the New Testament did not exist until some centuries later than these early actions of the first followers of Jesus. The normal vehicle of literature was a scroll, about the length of a single gospel. The Christians were among the first to pioneer the form of a book. A scroll was written on one side only, whereas a book – or codex, to use the technical term of the time – consisted of leaves of papyrus written on both sides, back and front, and bound together. In the second and third centuries of the Christian era the codex seems to have been largely a Christian speciality. It is suggested that a codex was easier for the itinerant messengers of the gospel to carry around with them. However, it was still a couple of centuries before a codex could be made large enough to take all the books of the New Testament, let alone those of the much larger Old Testament.

Books were expensive, and copying them by hand was laborious. In any case, in an oral culture where learning by heart came easily and naturally, the written word was less valued than the spoken word. In about AD 110 Papias, bishop of Hierapolis in Asia Minor, claims to have known presbyters who received the message directly from the disciples of Jesus. He gave more credence to the living voice than to books:

> I inquired as to the words of the presbyters what Andrew or what Peter had said, and what Aristion and the presbyter John, the Lord's disciples, were saying. For I did not suppose that information from books helped me so much as that from a living and abiding voice. (quoted by Eusebius, *HE* 3.39)

The Letters of Paul

The first Christian writings were letters, probably those of Paul, though some scholars consider the Letter of James still earlier. These were written to respond to specific problems put to Paul by the communities which he had founded round the seaboard of the eastern Mediterranean, or problems of which he had heard from messengers. So probably the first letter of all, to the Thessalonians, was written to explain to them how it was that Christians could have died, when Paul had taught them that Christ had conquered death. To the quarrelsome community at Corinth he wrote a whole series of letters, only some of which have survived, chiding them and urging them to put their differences behind them for the sake of Christian love. To Rome, a community he had not founded, he wrote in a very different tone befitting a letter written to the magnificent capital of empire. He needs their help for his projected mission to distant and unknown Spain, and hardly dares to give them any advice or guidance. He apologises profusely for his temerity in writing to them at all.

Official imperial letters were sent by a well-organised and efficient system of carriers. Only officials had access to this. Paul made use of his own messengers, who were probably travelling anyway in that direction. In making use of the widespread practice of writing letters he evolved his own variation of it, for there was no precedent for such long letters of admonition and guidance, to be read out to communities, nor for the specifically Christian greeting and blessing with which they begin and end.[2] It was not till half-a-century later that these letters were collected.

Clement of Rome 47.1, writing to Corinth in 96, refers to Paul's letters, and so does Ignatius, the martyred bishop of Antioch, a decade later. It is, however, not till the latest writing of the New Testament, 2 Peter 3:16, well into the second century, that a collection of the letters is implied, 'He [our brother Paul] makes this point *in all his letters*'. We do not know how the collection was organised. Did someone write round to all the Pauline churches, requesting them to send in copies of the letters? At any rate, it was not a total collection, for Colossians 4:16 mentions a letter to the Laodiceans which has perished totally. In the Corinthian correspondence Paul mentions (1 Corinthians 5:9) a previous letter which has perished, and a 'letter written in distress' (2 Corinthians 7:8), sent between the First and Second Corinthian letters which we do possess. There may have been others, too, besides these ones which Paul happens to mention. The first collection of which we have details was promulgated by Marcion in the mid-second century, containing ten letters, omitting the Pastoral Letters (to Timothy and Titus), thereby agreeing with most modern scholars who discount their authorship by Paul, but including Colossians and Ephesians which are also often denied to Paul by modern scholars.

The Four Gospels

The genesis of the remainder of the New Testament is more obscure. We hear tell of a couple of passages of the early tradition memorized by heart. Paul prefaces these with the claim that he 'received' them from the Lord and 'passed them on to you', using two technical terms of the rabbinic process of passing on the oral tradition (1 Corinthians 11:23; 15:3). He then slips into a vocabulary and style which differ slightly from his own, and show that he is quoting rather than composing freely:

> On the night he was betrayed the Lord Jesus took some bread, and after he had given thanks he broke it, etc.

> Christ died for our sins in accordance with the scriptures and he was buried and on the third day he was raised to life, etc.

These are presumably passages learned by heart by Paul himself, taught to his converts and memorized by them as the essentials, the institution of the eucharist, and the death and resurrection of Jesus. We are still a far cry from the written record of the ministry of Jesus given by the gospels. The work of the Form Critics, beginning with Karl Ludwig Schmidt in 1919, and Rudolf Bultmann and Martin Dibelius in 1921, has established that the component units of the gospels, stories, sayings, parables, were handed down orally in the communities, undergoing a certain process of development and elaboration typical of oral tradition, before they were welded into gospels. It has even been possible to establish[3] (from clumsy translation into Greek) that certain of the units of tradition were handed down originally in Aramaic.

The oral origin of much of the material is still discernible in the earliest gospel we possess, the Gospel of Mark, for Mark uses techniques typical of oral teaching, such as superfluous repetition, known in the trade as Markan duality. 'At evening, when the sun had set' (Mark 1:32), 'then, on that day' (Mark 2:20), 'when he was in need and was hungry' (Mark 2:25), are all phrases typical of oral teaching, which works on the assumption that much of what is said will escape the listener. A listener adverts to only a portion of what is said, and cannot look back to check, as a reader can. An oral teacher therefore often needs to say something twice, slightly more focused the second time, to get a message across. Mark also, just as the editors of the prophetic books, gathers together groups of Jesus' teachings, not necessarily in chronological order, groups of parables (Mark 4), groups of controversies with Jewish leaders in Galilee (Mark 2:1–3:6) or in Jerusalem (Mark 12).

There is general agreement that Mark was the first of the three gospels, Mark, Matthew and Luke, to be written. We do not know what specific reason or occasion led Mark to write his gospel. The usual reason given is that the original disciples, the original tradents of the tradition, were getting old, forgetful or dying out. But the quotation from Papias, given above, shows that the process of handing on information about Jesus orally was still lively and thriving in the second century. No doubt conditions and requirements varied in the different Christian communities, just as personalities would have done. Scholars generally date the gospel of Mark to AD 65–75. This conventional dating is a means of expressing that the preoccupation, especially in Mark 13, with the Fall of Jerusalem in AD 70 shows that it was written about that time. No one, however, can be sure whether it was written when the sack of Jerusalem was simply a menacing prospect (the Roman troops began advancing on Jerusalem in AD 66) or whether it had already recently occurred.

Careful reading shows the audience for which each of the gospels was written. Mark wrote for an audience which was familiar enough with Judaism to appreciate the force of the biblical quotations as evidence, but unfamiliar enough to need explanation of such customs as washing up to the elbow before eating (Mark 7:4), unfamiliar enough with Aramaic to need a translation of *Talitha kum* (5:41), 'young girl, get up'. Was his audience perhaps proselytes to Judaism, 'god-fearers', gentiles who were attached to the synagogue but not indigenous Jews nor yet fully committed to Judaism? Mark might have been chosen for his brilliant skill in telling a story, and his ability in organising the gospel story. Although the Greek he writes is fairly primitive and has been described as 'kitchen Greek', the sort of Greek which would have been spoken by slaves all around the eastern Mediterranean, he is a superb story-teller. His description of the unfortunate Gerasene demoniac, a massive hulk, too strong for anyone to master, deranged, gashing himself with stones and howling in the tombs, is memorable (Mark 5:3–5). The contrast between Peter, the hunky great fisherman, and the little wisp of a serving-girl who blows him away during the trial of Jesus is brilliantly witty (Mark 14:69–70). One of Mark's talents is to zoom in on a 'stage-prop' such as the cushion on which Jesus was asleep (Mark 4:38) or the horrifying, bloody head of John the Baptist (Mark 6:28). Another of Mark's talents is his ability to communicate with the reader; he is also a master of irony, writing on two levels, so that the actors convey to the reader more than they know themselves. When the Roman soldiers mock Jesus as 'King of the Jews', little do they know (as the reader does) the truth of their gibe. When the Roman centurion acknowledges Jesus as 'son of god' he has little idea of the depth of his state-ment. The interest in things Roman and the use of Latin loan-words (*centurio, denarius*) has suggested to some that Mark wrote at Rome, but these are features of the milieu which included the whole of the Mediterranean world. My use of 'milieu' or 'rendezvous' does not mean that I am writing in Paris.

Matthew, on the other hand, was clearly writing for a community sprung from Judaism. So he constantly stresses that Jesus fulfils the scriptures, that (in the first two chapters) he is son of David, a second Moses, bringing the Law to perfection (in the Sermon on the Mount). Matthew's audience is thoroughly familiar with Jewish customs like tithes and ritual purity (Matthew 23:23, 26), with the three Jewish good works of almsgiving, prayer and abstinence (Matthew 6:1–18). Matthew's community must have found that Mark does not give enough of the teaching of Jesus, so asked Matthew to include more of the sayings of Jesus. Matthew also illustrates them with a clutch of parables, narrated with his characteristic stark contrast between 'goodies' and 'baddies' (one who uses his talents, another who buries them; sheep and goats at the Last Judgement). While, however, being thoroughly Jewish, Matthew also warns that Christians will be handed over to sanhedrins and scourged in 'their' synagogues (10:17 – as opposed to 'our synagogues'?); so his readers were persecuted by Jews. One suitable community for which he may have been writing is Antioch, where there was a flourishing Jewish community, and where the followers of Jesus were first called 'Christians' or 'Messianists' (Acts 11:26). At Antioch after the Fall of Jerusalem the Jews were persecuted by the other citizens. If Matthew's community was a persecuted minority of a persecuted minority, they would need encouragement.

The community to which Luke seems to be directed was utterly different. Luke presupposes little familiarity with Judaism, and stresses that Jesus' message included the gentiles, right from the beginning (Luke 4:16–30). His whole style is far more sophisticated, both in the words he uses and in delicacy and allusiveness of his writing. He depicts not 'goodies' and 'baddies', but mixed characters who do the right thing for the wrong reason (the Unjust Judge, the Prodigal Son). He uses larger sums of money and warns against the dangers of wealth, which suggests that he is writing for a well-to-do audience. They are expected to understand about banking and interest rates (Luke 19:23), which would be far beyond Mark's limited world.

The extensive similarities between Matthew and Luke have led many to argue persuasively that both writers must have filled out the bare outline of Mark by drawing teachings of Jesus from the same collection of Sayings of Jesus. This collection of Sayings subsequently disappeared, but has been reconstructed in considerable detail by modern scholars.[4] If indeed it existed, it would provide valuable evidence of a pre-gospel collection. In itself it should perhaps not be called a gospel, for it seems to have no mention of the passion, death and resurrection of Jesus. The sayings recorded in this collection, nicknamed 'Q' (from the German *die Quelle* – the source), reflect a group that rejects the comforts of a stable society. One of the problems about this hypothetical document, which no one has ever seen, is to explain its disappearance. One would expect such a document to be carefully treasured by the early Christian community. Was it discarded by Christians because of its silence about the Passion or because of its rejection of society? Or was it simply not copied in Egypt, from whose arid sands have come most of the papyrus finds of recent years? If it existed, it could well be one of the 'accounts of the events that have reached their fulfilment among us' which Luke studied when preparing his gospel (Luke 1:1–3). Luke is normally considered to reflect its shape more closely than does Matthew.

From our point of view, the interesting point about the Gospel of John, which stands under the authority of the Beloved Disciple, is its independence of the other three gospels. It follows a quite different geographical and chronological pattern, showing Jesus visiting Jerusalem four times during his ministry, not just during the final week, as in Mark and the other two gospels. Instead of a host of miracles and many parables, John's Jesus tells no parables, and works a few, highly significant miracles. Some of the miracles (the Walking on the Water, the Multiplication of Loaves) are basically the same in all four gospels. Others seem to be different accounts of the same event (the Cure of the Royal Official's Son in John, similar to the Cure of the Centurion's Boy in Matthew and Luke). Still others are unique to John. The same is true of Jesus' sayings: some are the same, some different versions of basically the same saying, others quite different. The long Johannine discourses, with their elevated, meditative style and concentration on Jesus' personality, have no equivalent in the other three gospels. At all events John seems to represent a different stream of oral tradition, which overlaps occasionally with that which lies behind the other three gospels. There is just a touch of special similarity between the traditions behind Luke and behind

John in the narrative of the passion and resurrection (no high priestly trial, a similar meeting between the Risen Christ and the Eleven in the upper room).

It has long been conventional wisdom to see John as the 'fourth' gospel, the latest of the canonical four gospels, and some have even seen its purpose as being to supplement or correct the others. This presumption has recently been challenged,[5] and it is the independence of the Johannine tradition, rather than its earlier or later date, which now seems more striking. The principal reason for dating it later is the assumption that the greater stress on the dignity, and indeed the divinity, of Jesus should be regarded as a later development. It could, however, equally well be argued that different developments took place at different times in different centres of the Christian community. It is notoriously difficult to give a concrete date for any of the gospels. Ironically, the earliest scrap of text of any New Testament writing is a fragment of John, conventionally dated about AD 125, a date by which the overwhelming majority of scholars is agreed that all four gospels had been written.

The Text of the Bible

Variations in the Books Accepted

The problem of deciding which are the books of the Bible has already been mentioned (p. 8). Is the authentic and authoritative text of the Bible the Hebrew original or does the authentic Bible include the books of the Greek version used by the writers of the New Testament? Furthermore, the edges of the collection are fuzzy. Different traditions include different books (how many Books of Maccabees and what about *The Shepherd of Hermas*, the 'Psalms of Solomon'?), different chapters (Bel and the Dragon, Susanna, The Prayer of Jeremiah, Psalm 151), different verses (the Greek prayer of the Three Young Men in Daniel 3).

A decision between the Greek and the Hebrew arises repeatedly in the course of the centuries. Jerome reverted to the *Hebraica veritas* and insisted that only the books written in Hebrew have full authority, a decision picked up again by Luther and the Protestant tradition for doctrinal reasons. What, then, is the status of Ben Sira (Ecclesiasticus), a book originally written in

Hebrew, but received in a Greek translation, of which the vast majority of the Hebrew text was discovered only in the 1964 excavations on Massada? What would be the status of Paul's Letter to the Laodiceans (mentioned in Colossians 4:16, but never seen or heard of since then) if it were ever discovered? These are problems of the canon of scripture, solved for some traditions by the authoritative decision of the Church. The Roman Catholic Church made its decision at the Council of Trent in 1546, listing the individual books 'and all their parts' which are to be included. The Thirty-Nine Articles of the Church of England in 1562 took a middle position, excluding certain books, originally written in Greek, as doctrinally definitive but allowing them 'for example of life and instruction of manners'. A century later the Puritan Westminster Confession totally rejected these 'Apocrypha'.

Variations in the Text of the Books

Besides the problem of the canon there is the problem of the text itself: which is the authentic text of the Bible? We do not possess any text of any book of the Bible as it left the final author's hands or as the author corrected it (as a modern author correcting drafts of a printed text). There are plenty of varied translations, but it might be thought that they are all translating the same original Hebrew, Greek or (occasionally) Aramaic text. For well over 95 per cent of the biblical text this is the case, but again there are fuzzy edges. For the first millennium and a half of its life, before the invention of printing, the New Testament (and the Old Testament for nearly two millennia) was being painstakingly copied and re-copied, each time with variations and mistakes. Sometimes copyists made matters worse by correcting what they considered to be mistakes. Jerome, in the fourth century, already complained of the variety of texts, pointing out that there were as many variations as there were copies. At the Renaissance Erasmus attempted to reconstruct the text of the New Testament for its first printing, using only what we now know to be late and mediocre manuscripts of one particular type, the type standardized and approved by the Greek Orthodox Church. Since that time several great, ancient manuscripts have been found, which show how faulty this type of text was. In the last century quantities of papyrus fragments have been recovered from the arid sands of Egypt, much older and often less corrupted that even those great manuscripts. After the Second World War major finds were made in the Judean desert, west of the Dead Sea, which give us portions of the text of the Old Testament a thousand years older than any biblical Hebrew text hitherto known. These included a practically complete scroll of the Book of Isaiah, and the first Hebrew text of Ben Sira, known since it was translated into Greek in biblical times.

Most of the variations between all these texts are slight, for they were copied with extraordinary care and fidelity, but it is worth listing a few of the more striking variations in the gospels:

- Mark 1:1: In some manuscripts the verse ends 'Jesus Christ, *son of God*' in others simply 'Jesus Christ'.
- Mark 16:8: In some MSS the gospel ends here at the empty tomb; in others meetings with the Risen Christ are included (Mark 16:9–20).
- Luke 2:14: ends either 'peace on earth, *good will to* all people (εὐδοκία)
  or 'peace on earth to people *of good will* (εὐδοκίας) – a difference of one letter.
- Luke 22:43–44: The angel comforting Jesus and his drops of sweat 'like blood' in the Garden are missing from some MSS.
- Luke 24:12: The visit of Peter to the empty tomb is omitted by some MSS.
- John 1:13: Most of the best MSS read plural 'who *were* born' (referring to Jesus' followers), but many early Christian writers (Irenaeus, Tertullian, Origen) quote it as singular 'who *was* born', referring to Jesus.
- John 5:4: Mention of an angel disturbing the water of the pool is a later gloss.
- John 7:53–8:11: The story of the woman taken in adultery is missing from all the oldest MSS.

In these cases, which is the authentic biblical text? There is a moving account in the *Memoirs of Père Lagrange*, the founder of modern Roman Catholic biblical movement, of his distress at a textual decision of Church authority which he knew scientifically to be wrong. In 1897 the Holy Office pronounced that 1 John 5:7 was authentically part of the text: 'My distress was great. If the Holy See was setting up such barriers in the way of textual criticism, what were we to make of its views on matters reputedly much more serious? I took to the olive groves of Gethsemane [he was in Jerusalem] and immediately began a week's retreat, which brought me peace.'[6] In fact the decision of the Holy Office was later withdrawn.

Some editions of the New Testament choose one option, some another. Reputable scholars differ among themselves. One of the most distinguished of all textual scholars, Bruce Metzger, the chairman of the panel which produced the latest United Bible Society Greek text and the chairman of the committee for the NRSV, wrote a book explaining the decisions made by the panel for the UBS Greek text, *A Textual Commentary on the Greek New Testament* (Stuttgart, United Bible Societies, 1971). Occasionally, with the utmost courtesy, he supports a decision different from that of the panel of which he was chairman.

Biographies of Manuscripts

A few short 'biographies' of manuscripts will outline the raw material on which textual scholars operate. They are all interesting characters!

The Qumran Scroll of Isaiah

In 1947 a shepherd-boy, throwing stones on the shore of the Dead Sea, hit his target, a hole in a cliff-face, and heard the sound of broken pottery. Dad was summoned (for fear of evil spirits), a cave was broken open, and jars full of rolls of manuscript were found: the 'Dead Sea Scrolls', including a complete scroll of Isaiah. During the next decade, despite the Israeli War of Independence raging round that area, ten more caves containing manuscripts were found and a settlement. The scrolls were the precious library of the inhabitants of the settlement, hidden in the cliffs at the approach of the Roman army in AD 66 as it advanced to besiege Jerusalem. Most of the scrolls are now in the Israeli Museum, though some are in the Museum of Amman in Jordan. The scroll therefore dates from the time of the settlement at Qumran, 170 BC–AD 66, probably about 100 BC.

The Masada Scroll of Ben Sira

After the sack of Jerusalem in AD 70 the extreme militant party of the Jews, the Zealots, made a final stand in the great fortress-palace built by King Herod high above the western shore of the Dead Sea. This in its turn was captured by the Romans in AD 73 after two years of siege and a desperate last stand by the Zealots. Josephus tells us that the defenders committed suicide to a man, and when the Romans broke in they discovered only a couple of women, cowering in a bunker. In the ruins of the synagogue was discovered Chapters 39–44 of Ben Sira in Hebrew. Until then the book had been known only in a Greek translation.

The Magdalen Papyrus

In 1901 a former scholar of Magdalen College, Oxford, acquired at Luxor in Egypt and donated to his old College a fragment of papyrus. Papyrus is a form of writing material made from the soft, pithy stem of the papyrus plant which grows well in Egypt. Two layers of the plant are placed flat at right-angles to each other and then pressed flat. It takes ink well and clearly. On the Magdalen papyrus the stems at right-angles to each other are clearly visible, and the writing on both sides can be read easily, a few words from Matthew 26, verses 7–8 and 31. I was shown it in June 2004. To add to the significance of this fragment, two other fragments are known from the same codex, one now in Barcelona (containing parts of Matthew 3 and 5) and one in Paris (containing parts of Luke 1–6). They were all dug up in 1889 in Luxor, but sold separately. The handwriting and layout shows that this codex was written well before AD 200. If it contained two gospels, it probably contained all four, and is therefore evidence that there was already a book of the canonical gospels at that date.

Ancient Book Production

At this time scrolls were still the normal means of book-production. A scroll is written on one side only and rolled up. A codex has leaves written on both sides and bound together down one side. When and why did codices begin to be produced? They were originally rough and temporary notebooks, just two or four wooden 'leaves' (codex means 'block of wood'), bound together down the

side, the face being recessed a few millimetres to receive a coating
of wax, on which notes could be scribbled (and later wiped out)
with a sharp point.

As a form of book, with many leaves, it looks as though it was
invented, or at least popularised, by Christians. Of all the fragments of pagan writings from the second century hitherto found
only two per cent are written on both sides, so come from codices;
the rest are from scrolls. On the other hand, 99 of the 111 biblical
fragments from before AD 300 are from codices. Why did
Christians favour this form of book? Was it because they wanted to
put the four gospels together and no scroll would have been long
enough, or because codices were easier for Christian missionaries
to carry around?

Codex Vaticanus

Possibly the best of all manuscripts of the whole Greek Bible, this
was written in Egypt in the mid-fourth century, and has been in
the Vatican library since at least 1475. Comparison to papyri of the
early third century shows that it is faithful to the text current soon
after AD 200. It was carefully checked, and occasionally corrected,
by another scribe soon after it was written.

Codex Sinaiticus

This priceless fourth-century Greek manuscript was found in
1844 in the monastery of Saint Catherine's on Mount Sinai by the
German scholar Constantine Tischendorff. It is one of the chief
witnesses to the Septuagint, beautifully clear and legible. On the
grounds that the monks were not caring for it properly,
Tischendorff was determined to get it out of the monastery, and
– with a promise that it would be returned – persuaded the monks
to lend it to the tsar of Russia, their Protector, just so that he
could have a look at it. It was never returned, and in 1933 it was
sold by Stalin for a paltry sum to the British Museum (it is now
on show in the British Library). In 1975 a fire in Saint Catherine's
revealed another dozen leaves of the manuscript, which the Abbot
allowed me to examine in 1992. Theoretically these are now being
prepared in the monastery for publication, but in 2004 the
librarian told me that they will never be published till Tischendorff's slur on the monks has been officially denied.

Codex Bezae

This manuscript, containing the four gospels and most of the Acts of the Apostles, was presented to the University of Cambridge (in whose library it may still be seen) by the Renaissance scholar Theodore Beza in 1581. The interest of this one is that it is bilingual, written on facing pages in Greek and Latin respectively. It was written before AD 400, probably at Beirut, already an important centre for Roman law studies. The Latin text is particularly fascinating because it is much the best and fullest representative of the pre-Jerome Latin texts, the 'Old Latin'. The Greek also differs considerably from the conventional text, is often longer (especially in Acts, where it is some six per cent longer than the standard text), and may well be much older. After Luke 6:4 it adds the odd little story:

> On the same day, seeing someone working on the Sabbath, he said to him, 'Man, blessed are you if you know what you are doing; but if you do not know, you are cursed and a transgressor of the Sabbath.'

This manuscript often tends to brighten the text with slight emphases and exaggerations. However, the Greek text also contains a quantity of nonsense readings, which suggests that the scribe may have been more at home in Latin than in Greek. It is not easy to decide whether the Codex Bezae represents an older tradition than the standard, 'Alexandrian', text or whether it is a re-working of that text, but minute analysis of the text of Acts has led one scholar to the latter alternative. She concludes that it is 'a carefully crafted work of a skilful writer who was animated by a clear theological purpose'.[7]

Which is Correct?

In deciding between the readings a number of factors must be considered. The oldest text is not always the best, for a younger manuscript written in Egypt may have escaped a corruption suffered by an older text from Antioch or its ancestor. The most widely attested is not necessarily the best; the true reading may have been preserved by only a minority of manuscripts. Further, a scribe has sometimes 'corrected' his text for theological reasons, to express a more familiar theology, or has harmonized a reading in one gospel with the reading familiar from another. One principle is *lectio difficilior, potior*: the harder a reading is, the less likely it is to have been invented. Again, a reading which explains the others is more likely (if three manuscripts have 'the', 'then', 'ten', the most probable is 'then', which could be at the root of both the others). However, textual criticism is an art as well as a science,[8] and there is no question of learning it in one easy lesson!

TWO

A Process of Selection

The Gospel of Thomas

The four canonical gospels were those eventually accepted by the Church, not without some controversy, particularly over the Fourth Gospel. Irenaeus argues ingeniously that there had to be four because there are four points of the compass, four zones of the world, four beasts supporting the Chariot of God in Ezekiel's vision (Ezekiel 1). He was the first to suggest the equation of the evangelists with these four beasts, though not in the order which later became standard (*Adversus Haereses* 3.11.8: the lion is John, the calf Luke, the man Matthew and the eagle Mark). Some scholars, however, especially those of the notorious Jesus Seminar in the United States,[1] claim equal authority – at least as a source for the sayings of Jesus, though not ecclesiastical authority - for a fifth gospel, the Gospel of Thomas. One saying not contained in the synoptic gospels which has been emphatically accepted by the members of the Jesus Seminar as authentic is no. 42, 'Become passers-by', seemingly a gnomic counsel not to become attached to the world

This Gospel of Thomas made its debut – or perhaps, to be more exact, its come-back – on the world stage at the beginning of the nineteenth century. Three fragments of papyrus purporting to contain sayings of Jesus, discovered in Egypt, were published in 1897 and 1904 among the Oxyrrhynchus Papyri. Then, in 1945, an Egyptian peasant family, digging for fertilizer-soil, unearthed at Nag Hammadi a jar containing thirteen leather-bound papyrus books. There followed the various shenanigans invariably associated with such peasant discoveries in the Near East, murder, concealment, black market rackets (The supreme example of this concerns the Mesha Stone. Discovered in Transjordan in 1868, this crucial stone inscription provoked so much quarrelling between the French and the Germans about who should have it that the bewildered bedouin discoverers eventually blew it up. The scholarly world has had to rely on a provisional and imperfect 'squeeze' of the inscription). Eventually scholars established that this was a library of mostly gnostic texts, now written in Coptic, but the majority translated from Greek. Since they were discovered within sight of the Coptic monastery of St Pachomius, Helmut Koester of Harvard, one of the scholars most closely associated with the publication of the finds, plausibly suggested that they might have been buried by a monk on the publication of Bishop Athanasius' famous Easter Letter of AD 367 , which listed the canonical books of the Bible and ordered the burning of all apocryphal texts with heretical tendencies. The most convenient publication of the texts is *The Nag Hammadi Library in English*, edited by James M. Robinson (Leiden, Brill, 1977).

A Collection of Sayings

Among these texts is a full version of the Gospel of Thomas. It is not a gospel in the sense of a narrative, but is a collection of 114 'sayings of Jesus'. This has been treated by some reputable scholars with the respect which would be due to the Sayings of the Lord dubbed 'Q' (if it ever existed and were ever to be found). Among the first was the great Joachim Jeremias in the 1970 revision of his important work, *The Parables of Jesus* (SCM Press, 1972). He considers the form of parables given in the Gospel of Thomas as possible sources for the sayings of Jesus on the same terms as the form of parables given in the synoptic gospels. On the other hand the *Oxford Dictionary of the Christian Church* (1974 edition, p. 1370) coolly comments: 'It has been thought possible that it preserves a few sayings of the Lord not found in the canonical Gospels which ultimately go back to genuine tradition; but its contents hardly warrant the extravagant claims made for it when it first became known in 1959'. By contrast, Professor Koester claims unblushingly that 'the Greek (or even Syriac or Aramaic) collection was composed in the period before about 200 CE, possibly as early as the second half of the first century ... A comparison of the sayings with their parallels in the synoptic gospels [and 68 of the 114 sayings have such parallels] suggests that the sayings in the Gospel of Thomas either are present in a more primitive form or are developments of a more primitive form of such sayings' (*The Nag Hammadi Library*, p. 117). The controversy continues whether they reflect more directly the sayings of Jesus than those given in the synoptic gospels or whether they are later excrescences.

Some of the sayings are parables, eleven of which occur also in the synoptics, but four of which have no parallel there, for instance no. 97:

> The kingdom of the Father is like a certain woman who was carrying a jar full of meal. While she was walking on a road, still some distance from home, the handle of the jar broke and the meal emptied out behind her on the road. She did not realize it; she had noticed no accident. When she reached her house she set the jar down and found it empty.

The claim to be more primitive than the synoptic parables is supported by the absence of allegory. These parables are mostly simple images, teaching a single lesson. One-to-one correspondence of each element in a story to an aspect of interpretation, as in the Sower (Mark 4:13–20) or the Wheat and Darnel (Matthew 13:37–42 gives a 'key' to the meaning of each element), has been established to be a progressive growth. A parable starts simple and acquires more detailed meaning as it is re-told by later authors. Thus the parables of the Gospel of Thomas might be drawn from a source used by the synoptic evangelists, who in some cases have developed their sources.

There are four cases where sayings come in the same grouping in the Gospel of Thomas and the synoptics (one case is nos 92, 93 and 94 in the same grouping as Matthew 7:7, 6, 8).[2] This cannot be coincidence, and must show some link between the Gospel of Thomas and the synoptics. But it does not show in which direction the dependence lies. We cannot tell from this which came first, Matthew or the Gospel of Thomas. The link could, of course, have occurred at an intermediate stage of sayings, before the final composition of the gospel.

The Theology of the Gospel of Thomas
The theological angle of the sayings is, of course, different from that of the synoptic gospels. There is no mention of the Passion of Jesus (no passion-predictions, let alone an account of the Passion), and no expectation of a Saviour who will return at the end of time, as in the synoptic apocalypse (Mark 13; Matthew 24–25). In the Gospel of Thomas to the question 'When will the

new world come?' Jesus replies, 'What you look forward to has already come, but you do not recognize it' (no. 51, cf. 113).

A notable feature is that the sayings are very Christ-centred, returning again and again to the point that true understanding is to be found in Jesus. This is an emphasis different from that of the synoptic gospels. These have isolated sayings like Matthew 11:28, 'Come to me, all you who labour and are overburdened and I will give you rest' (parallelled in Gospel of Thomas 90), but from Mark it is clear that Jesus came to proclaim the Sovereignty/Kingship of the Father rather than himself. The Gospel of Thomas, however, abounds in such sayings as, 'I shall give you what no eye has seen and what no ear has heard and what no hand has touched, and what has never occurred to the human mind' (no. 17), or 'It is to those who are worthy of my mysteries that I tell my mysteries' (no. 62), or 'He who is near me is near the fire, and he who is far from me is far from the Kingdom' (no. 82). Salvation is not from any exterior influence; it is from the light which is within; so, when the disciples say 'Show us the place where you are', Jesus replies, 'There is light within a man of light and he lights up the whole world. If he does not shine, he is darkness' (no. 24).

There are some claims which go even beyond the Johannine claims: 'It is I who am the light which is above them all. It is I who am the All. From me did the All come forth, and unto me did the All extend. Split a piece of wood and I am there. Lift up the stone and you will find me there' (no. 77), or 'He who will drink from my mouth will become like me. I myself shall become he, and the things that are hidden will be revealed to him' (no. 108).

Reaction to the Gospel of Thomas has been very mixed. Pheme Perkins in the *New Jerome Biblical Commentary* (art. 67, #67) denounces the sayings as reflecting the gnostic spirit of the final editor. Larry Hurtado[3] finds the whole tone of the sayings objectionable, and repeatedly criticises them as 'revisionist', 'elitist', 'disdainful'. 'The Jesus of the *Gos. Thom.* is a talking head, whose whole significance and role consist in speaking the cryptic statements collected in this text' (p. 473). Three features, especially, would become suspect in later theology:

● A certain suspicion of the body: 'wretched is the body that is dependent upon a body and wretched is the soul that is dependent on these two (no. 87, cf. nos. 29, 112).

- A strange transsexuality: 'I myself shall lead her [Mary] in order to make her male, so that she too may become a living spirit resembling you males. For every woman who will make herself male will enter the Kingdom of Heaven' (no. 114). This may be connected with a baptismal rite of renewal, which could form the background for no. 37: 'When you disrobe without being ashamed and take up your garments and place them under your feet like little children and tread on them, then will you see the son of the living one, and you will not be afraid'.

- The introductory phrase, 'These are the secret sayings which the living Jesus spoke and which Didymus Judas Thomas wrote down. Whoever finds the interpretation of these sayings will not experience death.' Secret sayings, the penetration to secret knowledge, and salvation through knowledge alone were soon to become characteristic of gnosticism. Furthermore, 'Didymus' means 'twin'. The implication appears in the third century that Jesus had a twin brother called Judas Thomas ('Thomas' is the Aramaic for 'twin'); this would soon become unacceptable in the catholic tradition.

The Gospel of Thomas is considered by many to be the most important of the non-canonical possible sources for the Jesus-tradition. We do not know why it was not accepted by the catholic tradition, but we can say that if it had been accepted, the catholic tradition would have been somewhat different. It is certainly less weird than many of the more maverick non-canonical gospels which were current in the second and third centuries. Some of the sayings do seem slightly strange, but this strangeness would no doubt be diminished if they had become as familiar as the synoptic gospels, and had been as frequently commented over the ages as those gospels. Without sympathetic explanation, sayings from the synoptic gospels also can shock: 'Anyone who comes to me without hating father, mother, wife, children, brothers, sisters, yes and his own life too, cannot be my disciple' (Luke 14:26).

From time to time voices are heard proclaiming that such collections of sayings, such 'secret gospels', were guiltily suppressed by Christianity by secret and unfair plotting or pressure, a deliberately orchestrated campaign by the Church against the truth. Elaine Pagels writes, 'fifty years later [than

Irenaeus' denunciation of the gnostic writings in AD 180]
Hippolytus, a teacher in Rome, wrote another massive *Refutation
of All Heresies* to "expose and refute the wicked blasphemy of the
heretics". This campaign against heresy involved an involuntary
admission of its persuasive power; yet the bishops prevailed'.[4] She
suggests that the same fear of the truth was responsible the delays
in publication of the Nag Hammadi texts: 'Access to the texts was
deliberately suppressed not only in ancient times but, for very
different reasons, in the more than thirty years since the discovery [of the texts at Nag Hammadi in 1947]' (p. xxiv), as though
some undercover Roman FBI had orchestrated the delays. In the
second century it is true that choices were made, and that one
interpretation of Christianity became generally accepted as
'orthodoxy' while others gradually lost ground and withered away.
There was controversy but no compulsion. In the twentieth
century the true reasons for the delay were academic squabbling
and administrative stalling. (The Egyptian ambassador to London
once remarked to me, 'There is no hurrying your application. We
have a five-thousand-year-old bureaucracy.') Sensationalist
theories of secret gerrymandering are without foundation.

Other Non-canonical Gospels

It is, however, instructive to compare the Gospel of Thomas with
some of the other non-canonical gospels which were current on
the fringes of early Christianity. In many of these Christian piety
seems to have run wild. One example may be taken from the
second-century Infancy Gospel of Thomas, no. 4:

> After this he again went through the village, and a child ran
> and knocked against his shoulder. Jesus was angered and said
> to him, 'You shall not go further on your way', and immedi-
> ately he fell down and died. But some, who saw what took
> place, said, 'From where was this child born, since his every
> word is an accomplished deed?' And the parents of the dead
> child came to Joseph and blamed him and said, 'Since you
> have such a child, you cannot dwell with us in the village;
> teach him to bless and not to curse, for he is killing our
> children' (quoted by J.K. Elliot, *Oxford Bible Commentary*, p.
> 1320; more fully M.R. James, 1924, p. 50).

Other stories relate the child Jesus causing a salted fish to swim around, or making clay birds fly (M.R. James 1924, pp. 58–59). One can only be glad of the Christian discernment which excluded such stories from the canonical writings. They show a flippancy and irresponsibility in the use of the miraculous wholly absent from the miracles of the canonical gospels. They are more akin to conjuring-tricks than to the advance of the Kingdom of God. Another story which would be extremely influential in Christian art, leading to a whole series of splendid mosaic representations of the Descent into Hell, is about Christ in the underworld after the crucifixion:

> While Hades was thus speaking with Satan, the King of Glory stretched out his right hand and took hold of our fore-father Adam and raised him up. Then he turned to the rest and said, 'Come with me, all you who have died through the tree which this man touched. For behold, I raise you all up again through the tree of the cross.' With that he sent them all out, and our forefather Adam was seen to be full of joy and said, I give thanks to your majesty, O Lord, because you have brought me up from the lowest Hades' (*Oxford Bible Commentary*, p. 1322).

This imaginative scene is reminiscent of those apocalyptic works which were not accepted into the canon of scripture. The personification of Hades, Satan, Adam and the 'King of Glory' makes an attractive dramatic scenario which could mislead if taken literally. The identification of the tree of the cross with the tree of the Garden of Eden is suggestive of later romantic legends absent from the New Testament. Such imaginative representations of Christian legends, often over-stressing one aspect and undervaluing others, proliferated in the early centuries of the Church. As they have been rediscovered in the archaeological excavations or chance discoveries of recent years, it has become popular to claim underhand conspiracy theories: they were censored or treacherously suppressed by the Church. The true story is less conspiratorial: after a brief vogue they simply did not stand the test of time. Of gospels only Matthew, Mark, Luke and John were felt to be sufficiently expressive of the truths of Christianity to be read in Church and to be copied and re-copied

over the centuries, while others simply fell away and were forgotten. Some, particularly the more lurid scenes of apocalyptic,
left traces in art. Thus the skull and crossbones often depicted at
the foot of the Cross represented the skeleton of Adam, buried at
the foot of the tree of the Garden of Eden, whose wood later
supplied the Cross of Jesus. Others had to await the archaeolo-
gists' quests in the sands of Egypt and the libraries of Europe.[5]

Marcion Enters the Fray

The approach of Marcion, though related to that of the Gnostics,
was significantly different. His was the first serious challenge to
what was to become the Christian 'canon' or normative selection
of books of the Bible. Marcion was a rich shipowner – Tertullian
calls him *nauclerus* – the son of the bishop of Sinope, near the
Black Sea. Hippolytus tells us that his own father excommuni-
cated him for raping a virgin, but this may simply be standard
abuse. So the venerable Bishop Polycarp of Smyrna (martyred AD
160) calls him 'first-born of Satan' (Irenaeus, *Adversus Haereses*
3.3.4). Justin Martyr, writing in AD 150, says that he was alive,
active and successful at that time: 'he has caused many of every
nation to speak blasphemies' (*Apology* 26.5). He came to Rome
shortly before the middle of the century and made the Roman
Church a gift of 200,000 sesterces (one year's take-home pay for
300 legionaries). When his theological aims became clear, the
Roman Church returned this money to him, and he set about
organising his own parallel church community. In this he was so
successful that towards the end of the century Clement of
Alexandria (*Stromata* 7.17.106) numbers him among the outstanding personalities of the previous generation. Eusebius (*Hist.
Eccl.* 4.15.46) acknowledges that there was at least one martyr
from his community, and his communities remained strong
enough for Cyril of Jerusalem to warn his own catechumens
against mistaking a Marcionite church for an orthodox one when
visiting a strange city. It was a church with sacraments, catechu-
menate, presbyters, deacons and bishops. According to Bishop
Ephrem, they remained strong in Eastern Syria right up to his
own day; he died in AD 374. This remains the more remarkable
because of his rejection of all sexual activity: according to

Tertullian (*Adversus Marcionem* 1.29) Marcion would accept for baptism only virgins, widows and celibates.

Marcion's manifesto, *Antitheses*, has perished, or rather survives only in quotations from refutations of his views by orthodox ecclesiastical writers. One cannot always form a coherent picture by reading one side of a controversy, for controversialists will always pick out the weaker points of their opponents' arguments and present them in the least convincing way possible, no doubt omitting links which would make them more persuasive or at least less nonsensical. However, Marcion's views are tolerably clear from these extensive refutations, particularly the five-book treatise written against him by Tertullian. Clarity is added by quotation in ecclesiastical writers of excerpts from the carefully expurgated Bible which he sponsored.[6] His basic thrust was a rejection of Judaism, the Old Testament and the God of the Old Testament. It is not without relevance that his views would have been being formed in the decade after the disastrous Second Jewish Revolt against Rome (AD 132–135); this may account for his hostility to everything Jewish, even the Jewish God. Marcion's *Antitheses* expressed what Marcion saw as contradictions between the God of justice in the Old Testament and the God of love in the New. There seem to have been two principal problems which bugged him, God's punishment of evil and the suffering of Christ. The first of these problems is not unlike that of those Gnostic thinkers who found the existence of evil incompatible with a good creator; Marcion's problem, however, is not so much the existence of evil as God's punishment of it. The second of these real theological difficulties he shared with the Gnostics. It was perhaps typical of a successful businessman that he set about solving them in a practical way, by tailoring the basic texts of Christianity to his own ends. First we will outline (from Tertullian's refutation) the basic parameters of his thought, and then we will see how he tailored the Bible to fit them.

The Well-springs of Marcion's Thought

1. The problem of divine punishment is a real one. There is indeed a real contrast between the severe God of the Old Testament who punishes, and Jesus who not merely forgives but searches out sinners to bring them back into the sovereignty of God. This is, of course, only a partial and slanted view of the God

of the Old Testament, for the God of the Old Testament is also a God of forgiveness. So much is clear from the exegesis of the name 'Yahweh' in Exodus 34:6–7, to which there are constant allusions throughout scripture. Marcion, however, sharpened the problem by fastening on various biblical texts:

> I am Yahweh, and there is no other,
> I form the light and I create the darkness,
> I make well-being and I create disaster.
>   (Isaiah 45:7, quoted by Tertullian 1.2)

Did God deliberately create disaster? Can the Father of Jesus Christ have sanctioned retribution, 'An eye for an eye', which Jesus explicitly abolished in the Sermon on the Mount (quoted by Tertullian 2.18)? Can love of others be restricted to fellow Jews when Jesus extends it to all people (quoted by Tertullian 4.16)? How can a good God be responsible for the two bears savaging 42 boys who had merely teased the prophet Elisha (2 Kings 2:24, quoted by Tertullian 4.23)? Or the massacre of the Amorites while 'the sun stood still' (Joshua 10:13, quoted by Origen, *Homily on Joshua 13*)? Marcion of course follows this up with claims that the God of the Old Testament is ignorant: God does not know where Adam is in the Garden when he asks, 'Where are you?' (Genesis 3:9). Similarly God needs to ask Cain 'Why are you angry and downcast?' (Genesis 4:6). Tertullian reasonably answers that God is not really asking, but speaks with a threatening tone (Tertullian, 2.25). The modern solution would be that the Yahwist tradition in the Pentateuch represents God anthropomorphically.

Marcion's solution, however, was that there were two Gods, one producing good, the other evil. He quoted, 'There is no sound tree that produces rotten fruit, nor again a rotten tree that produces sound fruit' (Luke 7:43, instanced by Tertullian 1.2). A God who produces evil must in fact be evil. The one, the Creator God, is the God of the Old Testament and of Judaism, the other is the Father of Jesus Christ. God the Father of Jesus is the unknown God proclaimed by Paul in his speech at Athens (Acts 17:23). 'The God of the Law and the prophets was not the Father of our Lord Jesus Christ. For the former was known, the latter unknown. While the one was righteous, the other was benevolent. Jesus was derived from that Father who is above the God who made the world' (quoted by Tertullian 1.27). This is not without analogy with Philo's teaching (*Leg. Alleg.* 3.51–54) that God (θεός) is the creative power who is responsible for goodness, and the Lord (κύριος) is responsible for punitive action. This problem of Philo and Marcion was the same, but their solution different, and there is no suggestion that Marcion was dependent on Philo.

2. Marcion's second problem was the suffering of Christ. If Jesus is divine, how can he suffer on the Cross? Does God himself suffer? According to Tertullian (4.12) Marcion held that it was only a 'phantasma' of Jesus which breathed out its spirit on the Cross (and Tertullian mocks the idea of a spirit breathing out a spirit). Marcion deduced from Philippians 2:7–8 that Jesus was only in 'the form of a man' (Tertullian 5.20). Had he taken on a genuine human body born of a woman it would have been dependent on the Creator God, so thoroughly evil, 'stuffed with excrement', as Marcion delicately phrases it (Tertullian 3.10). So he was never genuinely born of woman, but took on only a human appearance in the same way as the mysterious three visitors to Abraham in Genesis 18 (Tertullian 3.9), for this divine apparition shimmers between being called 'three men' and 'Yahweh'. Nevertheless, this apparent death had redemptive value, and Jesus descended to the dead and saved those whom the punitive Creator God had punished in accordance with strict justice.

Marcion's Bible

In order to sustain these interpretations Marcion was obliged to be highly selective in his acceptance of scripture. The two pillars of his theology were a ten-letter collection of Paul and an expurgated gospel of Luke. He rejected the Old Testament in its entirety, and all the other letters of the current New Testament, including the pastoral Letters of Paul (Timothy and Titus), as being infected with Judaism, and concentrated especially on Galatians, with its opposition between law and gospel, particularly in the first two chapters. Marcion accordingly places Galatians at the head of his Pauline corpus (the order is clear from Tertullian's discussion). There Paul proclaims assertively – against the envoys whom James, leader of the Jerusalem community, had sent down to Antioch and those Jews who were 'upsetting' Paul's converts in Galatia – that salvation is to be found only in 'his gospel' of faith in Jesus and not in the works of the Law:

> We have learnt that someone is reckoned as upright not by practising the Law but by faith in Jesus Christ; and we too came to believe in Christ Jesus so as to be reckoned as upright by faith in Christ and not by practising the Law, since no human being can be found upright by keeping the Law (Galations 2:16).

Marcion's true attitudes can, however, be seen most clearly in his treatment of the gospels. He accepted only that of Luke. Presumably those of Matthew and John were too obviously based on Judaism ('salvation comes from the Jews', says Jesus in John 4:22) and Mark went with them. Of the Gospel of Luke Marcion omitted the first two chapters, the birth and infancy of Jesus, since Jesus was not carnally born. These chapters are obviously shaped to show that the message of Jesus is the fulfilment of the Jewish hopes, and the fidelity of all concerned (Zechariah, Mary, Simeon, Anna) to the Law is heavily underlined. An alternative suggestion is that these first two chapters were not present at all in the textual tradition known by Marcion. It is true that the quotations given by Tertullian from Marcion reflect a particular tradition of the text, commonly known as the 'Western text', which departs from the normally accepted text. These two chapters, however, are obviously written by the same author as the rest of the gospel and are in integral part of it. The most economical hypothesis is that they were cut out by Marcion, rather than that he received the text without them.

According to Tertullian (4.7) Marcion's version starts off abruptly:

> In the fifteenth year of the principate of Tiberius Jesus came down to Capernaum. They were astonished at his teaching which was against the Law and the prophets.

The second sentence is a modification of Luke 4:31–32, which in the canonical text runs: 'He came down to Capernaum, a town in Galilee, and taught them on the Sabbath. And his teaching made a deep impression on them because his word carried authority.'

According to Irenaeus the opening of Marcion's Luke (he does not ascribe it to any particular author, nor does he need to, since it is the sole gospel) is even more explicit, inserting the italicised words:

> In the time of Pontius Pilate the governor, procurator of Tiberius Caesar, Jesus came into Judaea *from that Father who is above the world-creating god, manifest in the form of a man. He dissolved the prophets and the Law and all the works of that god who made the world.*

Jesus was not born, which would have been unworthy of him, but suddenly appeared, 'came down' [from heaven?] to Capernaum (Tertullian 4.7). Marcion continues to hammer home his message by minor but significant adjustments throughout the rest of the gospel. Among many others, he avoids mention of prophecies of Christ in the Old Testament, cutting out references to Jonah and Nineveh, the Queen of the South and Solomon in Luke 11:29–31, and the whole passage Luke 11:49–51, 'I will send them prophets and apostles ... so that this generation will have to answer for every prophet's blood ... from the blood of Abel to the blood of Zechariah'. He deletes the parable of the Prodigal Son, presumably because it suggests the return of Israel to the Lord. For 'the Law' at 16:17 he substitutes 'my words' so that it reads 'It is easier for heaven and earth to disappear than for one little stroke to drop out of my words', thus avoiding Jesus' endorsement of the Law. In accordance with his views on the bodily resurrection, at the appearance of the risen Christ in the Upper Room he omits the words in italics: 'Touch me and see for yourselves; a spirit has no *flesh and* bones' (Luke 24:39).

Marcion's Legacy

This brings home that perhaps the chief lasting importance of Marcion was the reaction of the wider Church. In rejecting Marcion's approach they saw the necessity of declaring what was and what was not part of scripture, of reaching agreement on a canon of scripture which was authoritative for the Church, both in the books which it contained and in the matter of the text of those books, for Marcion had not only cut out books of the scripture but had also cut up the books he retained! Part of the difficulty lies in the question itself. We can quite simply ask about a passage, 'Is it part of the New Testament?' Such a question was impossible until the time of Origen, for the term 'New Testament' as a collection of books did not exist. True, Paul had used the expression 'old testament' in 2 Corinthians 3:14, but it is clear that he does not mean a collection of writings but rather merely 'the old dispensation'; there is certainly no corresponding expression with 'new'. In fact all Paul's 8 usages of διαθηκη. clearly mean 'disposition', 'arrangement', 'covenant'. He can, anyway, hardly refer to a collection of writings called 'the Old Testament' unless he can also envisage a 'New Testament', which would have been absurd at that time. Hebrews 8:8 and 9:15 uses the expression καινὴ διαθήκη in the sense of 'old dispensation' and does not thereby refer to any collection of writings. In fact Marcion, with his detestation of all things Jewish, freely uses 'old' and 'new' of the two dispensations. It is even possible that he deserves the credit for inventing the expression 'New Testament', referring to a collection of writings, for Tertullian writes (4.6.1), 'He directs the whole of his work to setting up an opposition between the Old Testament and the New'. If he did initiate the use of 'New Testament' to mean a collection of writings – and it can also be understood in the sense of 'the old and the new *dispensation*' – Marcion's use of the term could well account for the avoidance of the expression 'New Testament' by ecclesiastical writers for another half-century. In the end, however, it triumphed, and the legacy of Marcion may possibly be to have provided not only the impetus to defining the books which belong to the collection, but even the expression itself.[7]

Tradition Versus Innovation

Conventionally, the period of the New Testament ends with the death of the last apostle as he finally closed his eyes. Raymond Brown, however, gives more latitude, for he holds that 'all the works eventually accepted into the New Testament were probably written before AD 150'.[8] But when was that, and why should this event conclude the New Testament period? The Second Letter of Peter is normally considered the latest of the writings of the New

Testament, and that was probably written well into the second century. It can hardly have been authored by Peter, who is traditionally held to have been martyred in Rome in AD 64.

Peter is often held to have been the first Bishop of Rome, and possibly even the founder of the Christian community in Rome. This bristles with difficulties, chief among which is that it is difficult to conceive that Paul can have failed to mention Peter if he was or had been at Rome when, in the mid-fifties, Paul wrote his Letter to the Romans.

The long list of greetings in Romans 16 does not suggest that there was any official approximating to a bishop at this time. In that list of greetings are included 'the household of Aristobulus' (Romans 16:10). Aristobulus, the grandson of King Herod, died at Rome in the late forties, and it is an attractive suggestion that among his household were Jews who had become Christians. They would therefore have a strong case to be regarded as the founders of the Christian community at Rome, some dozen years after the Resurrection. A more likely link of Peter with Rome is that he sanctified Rome by his blood and so became the patron of the Christian community there. It is obviously appropriate that the chief of the Apostles should be the patron of the chief city of the Empire.

The traditional link of Mark with Peter and Rome is similarly unfounded. It rests on 1 Peter 5:16, 'Your sister in Babylon, who is with you among the chosen, sends you greetings. So does my son, Mark.' It is acceptable that 'Babylon' is a cryptogram for 'Rome'. But the identification begs two questions:

1. Is the apostle Peter really author of the letter, or is the letter pseudepigraphic?
2. 'Mark' is a very common name in the Roman world. Is this Mark the evangelist?

It was certainly not considered necessary that all the books of the New Testament should have been written by members of the Twelve Apostles. How would Paul have crept in? More attractive is the suggestion of Karl Rahner[9] that the books of the New Testament are the foundation documents of the Church, expressing in writing the Church's own self-definition. They are normative for the Church's existence in the exactly the same way as the Twelve themselves were originally normative, representing the authentic oral tradition of Jesus.

A Second-century Kaleidoscope

At the beginning of the second century the variety within the Christian communities was kaleidoscopic. It is not surprising that there was disagreement about which writings were authoritative and which not. Already at the end of the first century differences among the followers of Jesus had been clearly foreseen. In Mark and Matthew Jesus' prediction of the future of the Church is full of the threat of false Christs and false teachers (Mark 13:21–23; Matthew 24:23–25), that is, of teachers and messianic figures with whom the writer disagrees. The Letters of John give painful evidence of a split between two schools of thought, each claiming to be the true heirs of the Johannine tradition.

There are different views unreconciled within the New Testament itself. The first major problem in the Christian community had been the question of the observance of the Jewish Law in Christianity. This problem had caused Paul's virulent split with Peter and the Jerusalem Church. In the next generation it no longer seems to have been so important. This is the implication of the Deutero-Pauline Letter to the Ephesians: 'You that used to be so far off have been brought close by the blood of Christ. For he is the peace between us, and has made the two into one entity and broken down the barrier which used to keep them apart' (Ephesians 2:13–14). Perhaps the strength of the Judaising party had waned with the dispersal of the Christian community of Jerusalem at the destruction of that city in AD 70.

Even so the legacy of Judaism continued, for in AD 374 St John Chrysostom still found it necessary to forbid Christians to attend the synagogue. The background of the Letter to the Hebrews must surely be a community which still hankered after the rites of Judaism. There can hardly have been agreement between communities like those which lived by the Gospel of Matthew and the Letter of James, a modified, Christianised Judaism, and the communities of Paul, who had rejected outright all observance of the Jewish Law. Where does the community which sponsored the Gospel of John stand with regard to Judaism? In that work, although 'salvation is from the Jews', nevertheless 'the Jews' is still the generalised name for the opponents of Jesus, and there is talk of those who accept John's high Christology being put out of the synagogue.

A Thousand-year Reign?

Eschatology, the teaching on the ultimate future of creation, was also a major problem. The fourth gospel finally settled for a realised eschatology: the second coming of Christ has already been realised in the coming of the Spirit into the Christian community, and there is nothing further of theological import still to occur; what (if anything) will happen to close down the system is of no interest to Christians. But even the fourth gospel does still show traces of a future eschatology, the sort of expectation of a second coming of Christ on the clouds of heaven evinced by the synoptic gospels (Mark 13; Matthew 24–25) and by Paul (1 Thessalonians 4:16–17; 1 Corinthians 7:29–31). The Book of Revelation (especially Revelation 20:1–10), and perhaps 1 Corinthians 15:22–25, attests a certain millenniarism, an expectation that there will be a thousand-year period of Christ's triumphant rule on earth before the end of the world. Although this was later to be rejected by the Church, it remained the world picture of theologians of the second century all over the Christian world, such as Papias, bishop of Hierapolis, Justin Martyr in Palestine, Irenaeus of Lyons, Melito, bishop of Sardis, Hippolytus of Rome and Tertullian in North Africa. It was not until Origen, Eusebius and Augustine that the picture changed and this reign of Christ came to be understood as the time of the Church, a 'spiritual' interpretation. This millenniarism is no doubt the reason why there was considerable doubt in the fourth century whether the Book of Revelation was part of the sacred scripture.

The Gentile Influx

The greatest problem of all, however, was the opening up of the Christian Church to gentiles, who had a completely different background to the Jews and 'godfearers' (gentile sympathisers with Judaism, attracted by such features as Jewish monotheism and morality, who had not taken the decisive step of fully embracing Judaism by accepting circumcision) to whom the message had first been addressed. They came to Christianity with their own mental baggage, and naturally tried to understand their new beliefs in those terms. There were great original thinkers among them, such as Basilides (fl. 125–155) and Valentinus (fl. 140–165). Basilides was 'a seminal thinker of great speculative power and sensitivity' (Frend, 1984, p. 206), and even grumpy St Jerome grants that Valentinus was 'possessed by nature of an outstanding intellect and had gifts provided by God' (*Commentary on Hosea*, 11.10). He taught at Rome, and the fact that he was almost elected bishop of Rome shows the influence and persuasiveness of his teaching. Unfettered by Jewish concepts of tradition and ecclesiastical discipline, these speculative free thinkers set about putting the truths about God, Christ, creation and evil into terms which made sense to them. By comparison, the unadventurous Christian apologists, struggling to remain true to what had been handed down to them, were of limited vision. Origen admits that one of these free thinkers, Celsus, described the proponents of what would later become orthodoxy as – alluding to Plato (*Phaedo* 109B) – 'frogs sitting round a marsh, discussing who was the most sinful among them' (Origen, *In Celsum* 4.23). At the end of the century Irenaeus more than any other figure became the standard of emerging orthodoxy, but 'Irenaeus would have been deeply offended had it been suggested to him that he was an original thinker ... Irenaeus is unlikely to have been embarrassed by the accusation that he derived all his theological insights from others.'[10]

For these philosophers of the neo–Platonic school there were two vital factors, knowledge and myth. Knowledge was to them the supreme good, whence the name 'gnostics', from γνῶσις or 'knowledge', whereas for Irenaeus, the champion of orthodoxy, faith rather than knowledge was the means to salvation.[11] For the gnostics it was knowledge which saves. Jesus is above all 'the Revealer'. This led them to regard the fourth gospel, with its stress on knowledge, truth, understanding and Λόγος, as their favourite: 'In the beginning was the Word and the Word was with God' (John 1:1). By knowledge God dwells in human beings: 'I have made your name known to them ... so that I may be in them' (John 17:26). Such championship by the gnostics made John's gospel for some time suspect to the more orthodox, and pre-vented its universal acceptance until well into the third century.

Plato had used myth, or more exactly 'story', to convey his understanding of reality and the world, most famously in the

Myth of the Cave (*Republic*, book 6). In Greek religion the myths of the gods were endlessly rich and varied. The same inventive and imaginative spirit licensed the gnostic philosophers to explain the world by creating myths around the Christian God. They built on a dualistic conception of the world, in which evil must be caused no less than good. And how could a good God create evil? For Basilides the answer was a dual origin, a distinction between God and Yahweh. God created good, and Yahweh created evil. Sprung from paganism, with its multiplicity of gods, the Jewish stress on monotheism does not seem to have been a concern for these thinkers; they were perfectly content with a multiplicity of divine beings. From God emanated Mind, Reason (Λόγος), Prudence, Wisdom, Power. From these emanated 365 heavens and the angels who created the world. But one of those was Yahweh, chief of the creator angels and cause of evil and strife. It was to liberate the world from evil that God sent his Logos into the world. For Valentinus the evolution of the world was equally elaborate, though different: God originated in Depth, whence emanated pairs such as Mind and Truth, Word and Life, to the number of 30 Aeons. The final Aeon was Wisdom, from whom the universe came into being.

A similar dualistic division solved the other major problem: if Jesus was divine, how could he suffer? The solution was the laughing Jesus. The thought and wording are obscure, but somehow the fleshly part of Jesus is nailed to the Cross while the living Jesus looks on laughing:

> And I said, 'O Lord, do I see that it is you yourself whom they take? Or who is this one, glad and laughing on the tree? And is it another one whose feet and hands they are striking?' The Savior said to me, 'He whom you saw on the tree, glad and laughing, this is the living Jesus. But this one, into whose hands and feet they drive the nails, is his fleshly part, the substitute being put to shame, the one who came into being in his likeness.' (Apocalypse of Peter, *Nag Hammadi Library*, 7.2.81, p. 344).

Or in another passage:

Yes, they saw me; they punished me. It was another, their

father, who drank the gall and the vinegar; it was not I. They struck me with the reed; it was another, Simon, who bore the cross on his shoulder. It was another on whom they placed the crown of thorns. But I was rejoicing in the height ... I was laughing at their ignorance (The Second Treatise of the Great Seth, *Nag Hammadi Library*, 7.2 56, p. 332).

This is possible through his dual nature, as another obscure passage attests:

Now the son of God was son of man. He embraced them both, possessing the humanity and the divinity, so that on the one hand he might vanquish death through being son of God, and that on the other through the son of man the restoration to the Pleroma might occur ... I know that I am presenting the solution in difficult terms, but there is nothing difficult in the Word of Truth (Treatise on Resurrection, *Nag Hammadi Library*, 1.44–45, p. 51).

It is evident that the passion narrative of the Gospel of John is the most sympathetic – or perhaps the least unsympathetic – of the four canonical gospels to this approach. Far from the gut-wrenching horror of Mark's account of the Agony in the Garden, the wordless final shriek on the Cross, John's account shows a Jesus in total control. He is not arrested till he has given permission and the arresting-party has acknowledged his divinity by falling to the ground at the 'I am' (John 18:5–8). Crowned as King on the Cross, he dies with dignity and only when he has signified his readiness with 'It is completed' (John 19:30). He dies nevertheless, and it is this which put John, suspect though he was in some circles, finally on the side of emerging orthodoxy at the end of the second century.

Amid this variety of sacred writings one importance of Marcion's theory was, as we have seen, to stimulate the Christian community towards a standardisation of the list of sacred books. Besides the Gospel of John some other writings continued to be regarded with suspicion in various parts of Christianity. In the West the Letter to the Hebrews did not win universal acceptance; this was partly because it claimed no apostle as its author, but perhaps principally because it refused forgiveness to those who committed serious sin after baptism (6:4–6). Such rigour would have made difficulties in the severe persecutions which assailed the early Church. Not all had the heroism to stand firm, and there was much controversy over whether apostates should be granted a second chance.

Until recently it used to be held that the first list of accepted books was the Muratorian Fragment, a list discovered in a seventh-century codex at Milan in 1740 by Ludovico Muratori, and held by him to date from the late second century. More recently, however, scholars have come to agree that this Fragment is a late fourth century eastern document. The first firm list now commonly accepted as authoritative is therefore the list given in the Festal Letter of Athanasius of AD 367.[12] This was soon confirmed by approval of the same list at the Councils of Hippo (393) and Carthage (397), both important Christian centres at that time.

THREE

St Jerome and the Vulgate

Rome and the Revision of the Gospels

The scriptural books which belonged to the *editio vulgata* of the Bible were listed at the Council of Trent. This was intended to be authoritative for the Church, that is, for 'Roman Catholics' who recognised the authority of this council. The actual authoritative texts of the books were published in 1590 under the patronage of Pope Sixtus V (so called the *Editio Sixtina*), with an improved edition two years later under Pope Clement VIII (the *Editio Clementina*). Like so many of the decrees of the Council of Trent, this was formulated in reaction to Luther, who, following Jerome, had rejected a number of the books commonly accepted in Christianity. Jerome, as we shall see, insisted on the *Hebraica veritas*, the 'Hebrew truth', and accepted as canonical only the Books which were originally written in Hebrew. Luther, largely for doctrinal reasons, reverted to this tradition, and it was in opposition to Luther's selection that the Council declared canonical the larger collection of books. Although the central selection is the same for all traditions within Christianity, the edges remained – and still do remain – fuzzy. Other traditions within Christianity, e.g. the Greek and Slavonic Churches, accept also other books and parts of books as canonical;[1] they are often printed as an appendix to the Vulgate.

'Everyone knows' that St Jerome, the irascible hermit of Bethlehem, was the author, that is, the translator, of the Vulgate. The real situation is more complicated and nuanced. The young priest Jerome came to Rome in 382, not for the first time. He had been born a Roman citizen in easy circumstances, able to acquire both an excellent education and his own library, in about 347 at Stridon, near the present-day Trieste. It is tempting, but unnecessary, to delay over his well-documented youth and education, for his letters are full, frank and fascinating. One incident must suffice. So devoted was he to classical learning that he needed to be rebuked by his famous dream, which it is worth quoting at length. It occurred in Lent 374, when his fasting had been used as a preparation for reading Cicero, and when he had been using Plautus as a relief from what he describes as the horrifyingly uncultured language of the Prophets:

> In the middle of Lent I caught a fever, which seized hold of my exhausted frame and left it no peace. Incredible to say, I was no more than skin and bone. They were getting ready for my funeral, since my body was so cold that the only place where the breath and heat of life could be felt was my still warm wasted chest. Suddenly I was caught up in spirit and dragged to the tribunal of the Judge. There was so much light and such dazzling splendour from those standing around that, falling to the ground, I did not dare to look. Asked my religion, I replied that I was a Christian. The Presider said, 'You lie. You are a Ciceronian, not a Christian, for where your treasure is, there too is your heart.' At that I fell silent, and amid strokes of the whip (for he had ordered me to be flogged) I was even more tormented by the fires of conscience, thinking over that verse, 'In hell who will give you praise?' However, I began to cry out and howl, 'Have mercy on me, Lord, have mercy on me.' This cry resounded among the blows of the whip. In the end those present knelt before the Presider and begged him to pardon my young age and grant me space to repent my error. Punishment could be exacted later if I ever again read books of pagan literature. In such a tight spot I would have been willing to promise even more, and began to swear by his name, saying, 'Lord, if I ever have or read secular books, I will have denied you.' At the words of this oath I was dismissed and returned to the upper world. (Letter 22, PL 22, 416–417)

Revision of the Old Latin Gospels

When Jerome came to Rome he was brought thither, straight from the Council of Constantinople, by two influential bishops, Paulinus of Antioch and Epiphanius of Salamis. He had already several publications to his name, including the later very influential *Life of Paul the First Hermit*. He had already tried his hand at translation and discovered some of the problems: a word-for-word translation is absurd, but a stylish translation deserts the original (*Preface to the Chronicles*). He asserts that he was brought to Rome 'because of some disputes between churches' (Letter 108, PL 22, 881). No doubt with his excellent Greek, his experience of the eastern Church and his knowledge of Rome, he was thought a useful go-between. Soon, however, he was working for the pope, and had formed – to judge from the tone of his letters (e.g. Letter 36, PL 22, 452–461) – a light-hearted and friendly relationship with him. He seems to have worked for Pope Damasus as drafting secretary, as well as answering scriptural questions for him. However, the frequent depiction of Jerome with a cardinal's hat hanging on a peg behind him is not only anachronistic but also an overstatement of his importance. (The lion who is frequently depicted lying cosily at his feet is also a mistake. It belongs not to S. Hieronymus at Bethlehem but to S. Gerasimos, whose hermitage was in the Jordan Valley. A lion at Bethlehem would be awkward; in the thickets of the Jordan it would be much more at home. I have myself seen a leopard shot in this area.) Jerome is never sparing of self-praise, and paints a vivid picture of the respect in which he was held at Rome: 'I was called saintly, I was called humble and learned. In practically everyone's judgement I was considered worthy of the Papacy' (Letter 45. PL 22, 481), despite which he was somehow not elected pope when Damasus died!

However during this stay in Rome he was entrusted by the pope in 383/4 with the task of 'restoring the New Testament to its Greek original' (Letter 71, PL 22,671). Since Latin had become the language of the Church in Africa and Italy, a variety of translations had sprung up, known as the Old Latin, highly diverse and of varied merit. The first translations of the Greek Bible into the Latin of the West had been made in the second century. Two centuries later there were 'almost as many forms of the text as there are copies', says Jerome. In fact his claim to have restored the New Testament to its Greek original is a typical exaggeration: he seems to have completed the revision only of the four gospels, for in his commentaries on the rest of the New Testament he makes no mention of a revision (and he is not one to hide his light under a bushel) and continually criticises the Latin translations on which he comments. They cannot be his own translations. However, as he expected and predicted in his dedicatory Preface to Pope Damasus (PL 29, 525), when his revision of the gospels appeared, howls of protest and accusations of 'sacrilege!' greeted his changes from the familiar old texts. Jerome's mildest reply was that there is no point in playing the lyre to a donkey (Letter 27, PL 22, 431); he did not take criticism lying down. 'If they don't like the stream from the purest fountain, let them drink the muddy puddles' (ibid.).

The revision, nevertheless, was undoubtedly a hurried one. He could be a slipshod worker: his weak eyes meant that he normally worked through secretaries, which makes his achievement all the greater. On another occasion he excuses himself for a rough piece of work by saying that he was struggling to dictate fast enough to keep up with his secretaries, and the messenger was impatient to set out: 'If my ability deserves no pardon, at least the time-factor does' (Letter 117, PL 22, 960). There certainly were improvements (e.g. Old Latin *pontificis* → *summi sacerdotis*; OL *rememorari* → *recordari*; OL *adpropriare* → *adpropinquare*), generally moving from a slovenly and colloquial Latin to a more scholarly and classical tone. H.D.F. Sparks points out that the later gospels are less thoroughly revised than the earlier ones, and that there is a lack of consistency in his treatment.[2] So of 'daily bread' he changes the Old Latin *cotidianum* to *supersubstantialem* in Matthew's version of the Lord's Prayer, but not in Luke's. In the testing of Jesus in the desert he changes the Old Latin *pinnam* to *pinnaculum* in Matthew's version but not in Luke's. Overall there is little attempt at consistency in the translation of a single Greek word by the same Latin word, which cannot all be considered elegant *variatio*, highly valued though that was by the rhetoricians.

Not long after Damasus' death the hate campaign at Rome against Jerome and his entourage of holy women – his detractors seemed to have wanted to suggest that it was his 'harem' – reached such a pitch that he was compelled to withdraw and set up in Bethlehem. He felt utterly betrayed, but still unrepentantly confident in his stance. As he leaves Rome he chides himself on not expecting such treatment. He writes, 'People kissed my hand, and abused me with a viper's tongue. With their lips they sympathised but in their heart they gloated. However, I know that one can get to heaven through a bad as well as a good reputation. Greet Paula and Eustochia; whether the world likes it or not, they are mine' (Letter 45, PL 22, 481–484). His memories of those last months in Rome were not warm, and later he mercilessly castigates the 'scarlet-clad whore of Babylon' and the 'senate of

Pharisees' (PL 23, 105). In Bethlehem he continued his monastic life, teaching his little group and writing his commentaries, both fascinating subjects which are unfortunately beyond our scope here, except in so far as they both enriched Jerome and fed into his work of translation. His retinue certainly continued to inspire him, for he frequently addresses them in the Prefaces to his commentaries and translations.

Bethlehem and the Hebraica Veritas

In Bethlehem he had plenty of opportunity to benefit from two important helps to his studies. The first was contact with Jews, the second was use of Origen's marvellous *Hexapla*. He had always had good relationships with Jewish scholars. In early life he had been tutored in Jerusalem by a Jew named Bar Aninas (Letter 84, PL 22, 745). *Quo labore, quo pretio!*, he says ('what labour, what a price!'). Bar Aninas obviously made him work hard. When Jerome bewails the price, does he mean the cost in concentration or in shekels? In Rome he remained in close contact with the Jews (Letter 26, PL 22, 430). He excitedly rushed off a letter to the pope when a Jewish friend arrived with books from the synagogue (Letter 36, PL 22, 452). Oddly, however, it does not seem to have occurred to him for some time to translate the Bible from the original Hebrew; so strong was the hold of the Septuagint. Now, in Bethlehem, he gradually realised that he must turn from the Greek Bible to what he came to call the *Hebraica veritas*, the Hebrew text of the Bible. He had long ago confronted the task of learning Hebrew ('How often I despaired; how often I gave up and in my eagerness to learn started again', *Letter* 125.12), and also acquired some knowledge of Aramaic and Syriac. Nevertheless, such a return to the Hebrew was nothing short of revolutionary. Both Origen and Jerome were acutely conscious of the mockery of the Jews, who used the differences between the Septuagintal text and the Hebrew to claim that the Christians had an inferior text.[3] Jerome mentions such mockery in the prefaces to his translations both of Josue (PL 28, 464) and of Paralipomena/Chronicles (col.1321). In Letter 37 (PL 22, 577) he instances a couple of passages which the Jews ridicule in the Septuagint, including 'Blessed is he whose seed is in Zion and whose servants in

Jerusalem', where a modern translation reads '... the Lord, whose fire is in Zion, whose furnace in Jerusalem' (Isaiah 31:9). This Septuagint version is indeed an egregious mistranslation, based on incorrect vocalisation.

In turning to the *Hebraica veritas* he was following Origen (c.185–252), the great scholar of Caesarea on the coast of Palestine. Origen has frequently been hailed as the greatest exegete of the ancient Church, combining sharp linguistic acumen with thoroughness and sound judgement. Later, however, he was considered a heretic, and Jerome writes a long and passionate letter (PL 22, 643–752), with his customary vigour of argument, defending himself for having read and learnt from Origen ('Does anyone want to praise Origen? Let him do so, as I do myself ... I have praised him as an exegete, not as a teacher of dogma, his mind not his faith, as a philosopher not as an apostle ... Let us not imitate his vices, whose virtues we cannot follow'). Like Jerome, Origen had also been influenced in his scholarship by the Jewish scholarly tradition, initially at Alexandria, the city of his birth and upbringing. Origen had undertaken what remains to this day perhaps the most awesome single work in biblical scholarship, the *Hexapla*. It was so massive (it has been calculated to have comprised 6,500 pages) that it was never copied and survives only in fragments.[4] The emperor Constantine ordered Eusebius, bishop of Caesarea, to have 50 Bibles copied, and some scholars have held that he ordered 50 copies of the *Hexapla*. This is, however, absurd, for they were intended for the new parishes of the growing city of Constantinople, and the *Hexapla* would have been quite useless as a lectern Bible, and could never have been made 'in convenient, portable form' (Eusebius, *Vita Constantini* 4.36). To Jerome the *Hexapla* was vital, and a major advantage of his presence in Bethlehem was that he was able to correct his text by using the *Hexapla* in Caesarea, a mere 50 miles away (*Commentary on Titus* 3.9, PL 26, 595); he claims to have corrected the whole text of the Old Testament by this work.

Hexapla means 'sixfold', and this was the Bible in six columns. The Septuagint had been translated for the sake of Jews in the Diaspora who no longer understood Hebrew, but once the Septuagint had been adopted by Christians as their Bible, it was abandoned by the Jews. Another translation was substituted, that of Aquila; but Aquila had such reverence for the text that his translation was so slavishly literal as to be – comments Jerome, with examples (Letter 57, PL 22, 578) – almost unintelligible.[5] It was therefore supplemented by another second-century translation, that of Symmachus. Origen would have been familiar with this three-columned Bible used in the synagogue at Alexandria. He himself added another three columns, the Hebrew in Hebrew letters and immediately to its right a transliteration into Greek letters. Then on the right of Aquila and Symmachus he added another version, that of Theodotion. He also occasionally compared it with other texts, such as one which had been found (as the Dead Sea Scrolls were found, many centuries later) preserved in a jar near Jericho.

Origen, however, was acutely conscious that one could not ride roughshod over the susceptibilities of those who were accustomed to the Septuagint text. It is typical of his wise judgement that his concept of inspiration left room also for divine guidance in the transmission of the text. He refuses to reject outright the copies of the scriptures, based on the Septuagint, which were in use in churches. 'Are we to suppose,' he writes, 'that providence, which has provided for the edification of all the churches of Christ through the medium of the holy scriptures, has not taken proper care of the needs of those for whom Christ died?'[6]

This flexibility would not be echoed by Jerome. He began by revising the Psalter from the Old Latin and the Septuagint for a second time. This revision was adopted by the Church in Gaul and became known as the Gallican Psalter; it was the version commonly used in the Latin breviary and elsewhere until the revision of the Psalter in 1945.[7] A previous revision, made during his time in Rome and known as the Roman Psalter, has disappeared without trace. The Gallican Psalter, despite its widespread and long-lasting use, cannot be said to be a successful translation. Like the Septuagint itself, it is far too respectful of the Hebrew word-forms, grammar and word-order, to the extent of often being unintelligible – or intelligible only to those who can discern the Hebrew word-forms beneath the Latin. A thousand examples could be given, e.g. the frequent cry 'confitemini Domino' is the translation of a Hebrew phrase meaning 'acclaim, acknowledge the Lord', but *confiteor*, like the underlying Greek implies confession of sin. It is astounding that Jerome, whose own style in his

letters is so limpid, racy and scintillating, could be content to
issue such a lumpy and awkward text. At this period he also
revised from the Septuagint what he called 'the Books of
Solomon', that is Proverbs, Ecclesiastes and the Song of Songs.
These revisions have all perished.

By 390, however, he realised that in order to prevent the Jews
continuing to reproach the Church with the falsity of its scriptures he must return to the Hebrew text itself and translate
directly from the Hebrew (*Preface to Isaiah*, PL 28, 774). Translation into Latin of a translation from Hebrew into Greek would
not suffice. So he began his greatest and most lasting work, not to
be completed till 404. 'With full knowledge and deliberation I put
my hand in the fire', he says, knowing the unpopularity this would
bring, and only asking the biased (*fastidiosus*) reader not to con-
demn his work unread (PL 28, 772–3). Both his approach and the
care he devoted to the different books varies considerably. The
first books translated, Samuel and Kings, are considerably more
literal than the final books; in the preface to Samuel and Kings he
vigorously defends the literalness of the translation. On the other
hand Judges, one of the last books, is not far from being a paraphrase. Secondly, in the matter of style he was perfectly capable of
flights of high rhetoric, but in his translation he deliberately
avoids them: 'A version made for the use of the Church', he
writes, 'even though it may possess a literary charm, ought to dis-
guise it and avoid it so far as possible, in order that it may not
speak to the idle schools and few disciples of the philosophers, but
may address itself rather to the entire human race' (Letter 49.4).
The translations are deliberately straightforward and simple,
retaining the bone-structure of the original Hebrew. This is the
secret of the quiet dignity and lasting quality of his translation
and of the distinctively Christian Latin which he created.

The extent to which he was preoccupied with the Jews – not to
mention the speed with which he could work – is shown by the
fact that he took so much less trouble with parts of the scripture
which were not regarded by the Jews as canonical. In his preface
to the Book of Tobit (of which he had only an Aramaic text) he
admits to Bishop Heliodorus, who had asked for the translation,
that it was an entirely oral translation: 'I have fulfilled your
wishes, but not to my own satisfaction. Since Aramaic is close to
Hebrew, I found someone highly skilled in both languages and

snatched the work of one day. Whatever he expressed in Hebrew I, having engaged a secretary for this, expressed in Latin words' (PL 29, 24–26). The Book of Judith got even shorter shrift. He consented to translate it only because the Synod of Nicaea 'is said to have reckoned it among the sacred books'. So 'putting aside my extremely pressing occupations, I gave it one little night's work (*unam lucubratiunculam*), translating it rather sense for sense than word for word' (PL 29, 39).

He was right about the resistance to change and the consequent unpopularity of the translation. The great St Augustine, bishop of Hippo, was rash enough to suggest to Jerome that on ecumenical grounds he would have preferred a translation based on the Septuagint, since the return to the Hebrew would drive one further wedge between eastern and western Churches. Before concluding the letter with fulsome compliments and praise, he went on to describe the tumult provoked in North Africa by a reading from Jerome's translation of the Book of Jonah:

> A certain bishop, one of our brethren, having introduced in the church over which he presides the reading of your version, came upon a word in the book of the prophet Jonah, of which you have given a very different rendering from that which had been of old familiar to the senses and memory of all the worshippers, and had been chanted for so many generations in the church.[8] Thereupon arose such a tumult in the congregation, especially among the Greeks, correcting what had been read, and denouncing the translation as false, that the bishop was compelled to ask the testimony of the Jewish residents (it was in the town of Oea). They, whether from ignorance or from spite, answered that the words in the Hebrew manuscript were correctly rendered in the Greek version and in the Latin one taken from it. What further need I say? The man was compelled to correct your version of that passage as if it had been falsely translated (Augustine, Letter 71, p. 327).

Needless to say, this provoked a furious reply from Jerome, who complained that a previous (unanswered) letter from Augustine seems to have become known all over Rome before it was known to Jerome, and twice asking Augustine to 'desist from annoying an old man who seeks retirement in his monastic cell'.[9] To Augustine's polite concluding suggestion that he is ready to accept from Jerome any correction of scriptural interpretations Jerome replies that he has never read Augustine's works with attention and has few of them, 'which if I were disposed to criticise, I could prove to be at variance, I shall not say with my own opinion (for I am nobody) but with the interpretations of the older Greek commentators' (among Augustine's letters, Letter 72).

The Completion of the Vulgate: A Pandect

In the final section of his work *De Viris Illustribus* (*On Famous Men*), which of course includes himself, Jerome claims 'I have translated the New Testament, faithful to the Greek' and 'I have translated the Old Testament in accordance with the Hebrew'. It will be clear from the above that each of these statements is an exaggeration. Because of his preoccupation with the *Hebraica veritas* he did not touch the Book of Wisdom nor Ecclesiasticus (Ben Sira), Baruch and 1–2 Maccabees, which were available only in Greek and were considered apocryphal by the Jews, though it was Jerome who coined the word 'apocryphal'. Jerome's choice was not without ecclesiastical support, for the Festal Letter of Athanasius lists Baruch among canonized books, but Wisdom and Ben Sira only in a second category of books 'appointed by the ancestors to be read to those who newly join us and want to be instructed in the word of piety' (no mention of Maccabees). In the New Testament he did not work on the Acts of the Apostles, the Letters or the Book of Revelation, let alone the *Didache* and the *Shepherd* of Hermas, two books also mentioned among the books 'to be read', but later dropped from the canon. The Latin text therefore still needed to be completed.

When this occurred we do not know. The first mention of a 'pandect'(from παν δεχεσθαι, which might be translated 'an omnium-gatherum', an 'everything-container') is in Cassiodorus, who mentions three pandects, one in nine volumes and two each in a single volume containing all the books of Old and New Testaments. These were produced at Vivarium near Naples in his house for the study of religious literature in the late sixth century.[10]

The first actual pandect we possess, however, is the Codex Amiatinus, produced at Bede's double monastery at Wearmouth and Jarrow. Bede's monastery was an impressive centre of learning. Bede's own scholarship was staggering, and his exegetical works draw effortlessly upon a wide variety of classical and ecclesiastical authors, Pliny, Josephus, Isidore, Adamnan, as well as Jerome and Augustine. His abbot, Ceolfrid, was extraordinarily open to the wider world, and brought to this cold and remote corner of Northumberland stained-glass artists and the papal arch-cantor from Rome to instruct the monks. Cold it may have been, but cultured also: it will be remembered that King Alfred, a contemporary of Bede, sadly remarked that it was difficult to find a priest north of the Humber who could write a decent Latin letter, and south of the Humber impossible. Bede also says that Abbot Ceolfrid doubled the size of the library. Among his most striking acquisitions must have been Cassiodorus' larger pandect, for Bede attests that he has seen one of its illustrations (*vidimus*, he says, PL 91, 454), and Bede lived his whole life within the monastery, leaving it only twice to journey to Hexham and York.

Three further pandects were then made at Wearmouth and Jarrow, probably before 700, one for each monastery (both of which have perished). The third was to be presented to the pope (PL 94, 725), but Abbot Ceolfrid died on the way when in 715 he was taking it to Rome. It is now in Florence, a magnificent volume, normally carried by at least two men and said (curiously) to weigh as much as a full-grown female Great Dane.[11] The skins of more than 500 calves would have been required for each of the three volumes. To be able to spend 1,500 calves on books bespeaks considerable wealth! Although its pattern of illustration is modelled on Cassiodorus' pandect, the Amiatinus uses Jerome's translation, as opposed to the 'older' form of the text of Cassiodorus'. The 2000 pages of text were written out by seven different scribes, all of the same English school. As might be expected, the fine illustrations, though English work, also betray Italian influence; the link between Rome and this northern monastery was clearly strong and fruitful.

FOUR

The Bible in English

Before the Norman Conquest

From the Roman Empire onwards Latin was the only written language of the West. Not only the Bible but all literature was in Latin. Boniface, the monk from Devon who brought Christianity to Germany, wrote his letters in Latin not only to the pope in Rome (whose Latin was so rough that Boniface, a stylish classicist, had difficulty understanding it) but also to his friends at home in England, to the bishop of Winchester, to the monks of Wearmouth and to the nuns of Minster in Thanet. The first steps towards putting the Bible into English seem to have been taken by the Venerable Bede. Before Bede we know only of paraphrases. The tradition of paraphrase of the text, rather than translation, is enshrined in the poem of Caedmon and *The Dream of the Rood*. Bede recounts (*Hist. Eccl.*, 5.24) how Caedmon, an unlettered labourer at the monastery of Whitby, was commanded in a dream to sing of the creation. His nine-line poem, marked by the strong rhythm and alliteration of Old English poetry, is, of course, derived from the account in Genesis; it is not in any sense a translation. The anonymous *Dream of the Rood* is another, longer (some 150 lines) triumphant masterpiece of Old English, in which the tree of the Cross sings of its experience in bearing the warrior Saviour, a scintillating application of the Anglo–Saxon heroic tradition to the biblical story.

Bede's disciple and biographer, Cuthbert, claims that Bede translated the Gospel of John up to John 6:9. Cuthbert tells us that he finished this on his deathbed, but it has not survived. Perhaps his literary executors judged it unready for dissemination. In the following centuries, however, we do have evidence for tentative beginnings, centred on those parts of the Bible which were most in use, the gospels and the psalms. These tentative beginnings were word-for-word translations written over the Latin words (so called 'glosses') as aids to the reader needing guidance through the Latin text. Two very early examples are the Surtees Psalter,[1] an eighth-century manuscript with the words written over the Latin in the Northumbrian dialect, and the magnificent Paris Psalter,[2] containing a prose version of the psalms in the West Saxon dialect, made possibly under the leadership of King Alfred. The style is similar to Alfred's translation of Boethius. The most important figure in translation into the vernacular before the Norman Conquest is, however, Aelfric of Winchester (made abbot of Eynsham in 1005), who provided a highly abbreviated form of the Pentateuch and most of the historical books of the Old Testament.[3] However, even he, in the Preface to his *Lives of the Saints*, writes, 'I do not promise to write very many in this tongue because it is not fitting, lest peradventure the pearls of Christ be had in disrespect'; he did not really believe that the scriptures should be available to the laity, a view which would have a long and important history. The crown of pre-Conquest translations is the West Saxon Gospels, a powerful translation of all the gospels which exists in five manuscripts, one of which claims Aelfric as author (*ego Aelfricus scripsi hunc librum*). A charming feature of the book is its development of compound words where no English word yet exists, for example 'mild-heortnesse' for 'mercy' and 'blod-ryne' for 'haemorrhage'.

The Norman Conquest

Such developments were abruptly halted by the Norman Conquest of England. Sixty years after the Conquest William of Malmesbury laments, 'At the present time there is neither duke, bishop nor abbot who is English. Foreigners are corroding the guts of England, and there is no hope of an end to this misery.' Only the French-speaking aristocracy could afford books, and their language remained Norman French until the Hundred Years War against France turned French into the language of the enemy, and English suddenly regained its confidence. One might say that the most lasting consequence of the battle of Agincourt was this new confidence in the English superiority to French. In 1322 parliament had prescribed that 'all lords, barons, knights and honest men of good towns must exercise care and diligence to teach their children the French language'. After Agincourt this changed. Henry V (1387–1422) is the first king of England since the Conquest of whom we possess a letter written in English, and the delightful scene at the end of Shakespeare's *Henry V* of the young king learning French from the Princess of France, may well be true reflection of his ignorance of the language. On the other hand, lawsuits were conducted in English from 1362, and the speech for the opening of parliament is in English from that date.

Standards of religious education were scandalously low, and with the specialisation of university studies theology was becoming more and more abstruse, more and more the province of the learned clergy. In 1222 the Council of Oxford required that priests should be able at least to understand the Latin formula of eucharistic consecration, but in the same year a Visitation of Salisbury shows that five in seventeen parish clergy were incapable of this.[4] In 1300 a copy of the Vulgate was so expensive that few individuals apart from higher clergy possessed one. Perhaps the most celebrated story is that of Lewis de Beaumont, the aristocratic Prince Bishop of Durham in 1317. Greystanes the Chronicler[5] complains that he was illiterate, giving the example that he stumbled so badly over the Latin words *metropolitice* and *in aenigmate* that he eventually expostulated in his Norman French, 'Par Seynt Louis, il ne fu pas curtays, qui cest parole escrit' (By St Louis, he was no gentleman who wrote that word).

Such clergy can hardly have been in a position to expound the Latin Bible to their flocks. There were, of course, other methods than reading by which the laity could receive their knowledge of the Bible. Significant is the story of the ploughman who confessed to the priest, 'Sir, I believe in Jesu Christ, which suffered death and harrowed hell'.[6] He had not heard of the *Pater Noster*, but knew of the harrowing of hell, whose dramatic visual properties made it a particularly popular subject for wall paintings. There was also, of course, a host of paraphrases and meditations on the Bible. Quite outstanding, therefore, was the early fourteenth-century psalter of Richard Rolle, the North Yorkshire hermit. This is a translation (e.g. 'thou that makes gostis thin aungels and thine minystres fire brennand' for Psalm 103:5) of the psalms and certain Old Testament canticles which he made for the recluse Margaret Kirkby, who presumably knew no Latin.

In this England was lagging behind some of the continental countries. In Germany translations and texts seem to have advanced at about the same pace. Interlinear glosses had been introduced, primarily as a means of study and understanding. The psalms are the stuff of Christian prayer, sung daily in countless religious communities; it was therefore important that the beginner should understand them. Just as the psalter was the first part of the Bible translated into Anglo-Saxon, so the monk and teacher Notker Labeo of Sankt Gallen made an interlinear gloss of the psalter into German in about 1000. Other translations of the psalter in the Benedictine monastic schools were probably associated with the schooling of novices (e.g. as suggested by fragments already from the ninth century in the Abbey of Reichenau). Similarly in the twelfth century such fragmentary translations, whose exact rendering of the Latin words suggests school use, have been found in convents of Dominican sisters and Cistercians. In 1260 an inquisitor found 'a certain unlettered countryman who used to recite Job word for word [presumably in German rather than Latin], and many others who knew the whole New Testament perfectly'.[7] An important new step was taken in the fourteenth century in the great work of Marchwart Biberli (c. 1265–1330), the Dominican lector of Zurich, who translated first the psalter and then the whole Bible, at a time more or less contemporary with the Wycliffian translation. His work is both exact and poetic, though his aims were primarily devotional and educational. His care was principally for students and religious in Zurich itself, and copies appear only in the Zurich area until 1360. In Italy 'substantial parts' of the Bible had been translated by 1250,[8] and in France a complete translation of the Bible existed by 1280.

In eastern Europe the origin of translation into the vernacular seems to have been liturgical rather than educational. Christianity was brought to the Slav countries (more specifically Moravia or, in more recent nomenclature, Poland, Hungary and Czechoslovakia) from Constantinople by the brothers Cyril and Methodius. They saw the importance of translation into the vernacular. There was as yet no writing or alphabet, but they immediately set about forming the alphabet now called Glagolitic or Cyrillic, more or less the modern Russian alphabet. In the teeth of opposition from the episcopate to the west of them, in Bavaria, they succeeded in obtaining permission in 869 from Pope Hadrian II to celebrate the liturgy in Slavonic; the scriptural readings were to be proclaimed first in Latin, then in Slavonic. According to the *Vita Methodii*, Methodius translated the whole Bible into Slavonic in the six months March to October 884. Again, it is hard to envisage that he completed this vast task in so short a time, and these were probably only liturgical extracts. In any case, the translation has disappeared.

Wyclif's Bible

The work of John Wyclif (c. 1320–1384) was therefore a major advance in biblical translation. Owing to its circumstances it acted also as a major deterrent of further advance. Wyclif was primarily a philosopher, described by his contemporary Henry Knighton as 'a doctor of theology most eminent in his day. In philosophy he was considered second to none, in scholarly learning incomparable.'[9] He was a great Oxford figure, master of Balliol and later warden of Canterbury Hall, sufficiently respected there for the Oxford establishment to close ranks in his defence (the chancellor at first refused to publish his condemnation, and the university suspended an Irish Cistercian who preached against his views). He lectured, unusually, on the whole Bible, and held the Bible to be the only source of true doctrine. He fulminated mercilessly against the corruption of the papacy:

> A man may be reputed Vicar of Christ by all human solemnity, rite and reputation and yet be a fearful devil, as it is not beyond belief in the case of Gregory XI and his like. For if a man used the tithes and goods of the English poor to marry off his nephew to an heiress, and supported the families of many of his kinsfolk in worldly pomp, and bought his brother out of just imprisonment and had many thousand men killed for worldly gain, who can doubt that he was a perpetual heretic and never a head or member of mother church?[10]

By contrast, the scriptures are open to all, and a source of truth and salvation to all. No ecclesiastical authority has a monopoly of interpretation. Wyclif urges:

> To believe solidly in the faith of scripture and to believe no one else on any topic except to the extent to which he bases himself on scripture. Even the lord Pope, or any other grandee, may be ignorant of the sense of scripture and, in a greedy quest for wealth, interpret it in a sense contrary to

Christ. But the faithful whom Christ calls in meekness and humility of heart, whether they be clergy or laity, male or female, bending the neck of their inner man to the logic and style of scripture, will find in it the power to labour and the wisdom hidden from the proud.[11]

It was primarily his political views which drew the fire upon him, his contention that both secular and ecclesiastical jurisdiction depended on being in a state of grace, with its consequence that unworthy office-holders deserved no obedience. It was only after this doctrine was condemned by the pope in 1377 that he became more extreme and began to teach that neither papal authority nor the vowed religious life had adequate foundation in scripture (it was the friars who were primarily instrumental in his condemnation), and to teach also against the philosophical basis of the doctrine of transsubstantiation. The translation of the Bible seems to have been almost an afterthought, for years later Archbishop Arundel wrote to the Pope in 1412, 'to fill up the measure of his malice he devised the expedient of a new translation of the Scriptures'. The work of translation is attributed to him by the continuator of Knighton's *Chronicle*: 'This Master John Wyclif translated from Latin into English the Gospel that Christ gave to the clergy and doctors of the Church so that they might administer it conveniently to the laity ... and so the pearl of the gospel is scattered abroad and trodden underfoot by swine'. Knighton considered, therefore, that the gospel had been given primarily and directly only to the clergy; the laity should receive it only through them. Jan Hus, the contemporary Czech reformer, had also heard of Wyclif's translation: 'It is said by the English that Wyclif translated the whole Bible from Latin into English'. In fact, however, the translation itself was done by one, possibly two, of Wyclif's disciples, rather than Wyclif himself (Nicholas of Herford and perhaps John Treviso); it is a mere presumption that he stands behind it. The thirst for such a translation, however, is clear from its popularity. Despite the banning orders against it, over 200 copies still exist in manuscript.

A match was put to the tinder by the appeal to his theological position made by the frightening but ultimately unsuccessful Peasants' Revolt of 1382. Such a revolt against established authority received the nickname of 'Lollardy', and whether it was considered more evil from the political or from the religious point of view, Wyclif was considered its high priest. Wyclif was expelled from Oxford and withdrew to his living of Lutterworth, under the nearby protection of his patron, John of Gaunt, the powerful duke of Lancaster, in Leicester Castle. John of Gaunt was sufficiently committed to him and his ideals – and sufficiently aware of the world beyond England – to speak in the House of Lords against the bill to suppress the English Bible: 'We will not be the dregs of all, seeing that other nations have the Law of God, which is the Law of our faith, written in their own language'.[12] So at Lutterworth Wyclif remained unmolested until his death; it was only half a century later that his bones were dug up and burnt as heretical.

The most significant element of the aftermath to Wyclif is the near hysteria which his political views engendered, and the consequent, though illogical, blockage on all translation of the Bible into English. Translation into English was regarded as the symbol of independence of authority, the breaking wave of the groundswell of discontent which had shown itself in the Peasants' Revolt. Both secular and ecclesiastical authorities appreciated this significance: it was an appeal to private judgement, a proclamation that all should have the word of God directly available to them, rather than direct access to the word of God remaining in the hands of an oligarchy who understood and read Latin, and all others having to rely on receiving it through them. In this sense Wyclif has rightly been called 'the morning star of the Reformation',[13] and in England translation of the Bible into the vernacular carried a whiff of Lollardy. Wyclif himself died in 1384, but Lollardy continued, merging seamlessly into the Lutheran Reformation. The fear and the resulting persecution of Lollardy continued throughout the fifteenth century. In 1401 the statute *De Heretico Comburendo* introduced the death penalty for heresy, soon after put into effect on the Lollard William Sawtry and others. A turning-point was reached with the Constitutions of Oxford in 1407, when Archbishop Arundel finally forbade all unauthorized translation: 'We therefore resolve and ordain that no one henceforth on his own authority translate any text of holy scripture into the English or any other language by way of book, pamphlet or tract, and that no book, pamphlet or tract of this kind, whether already recently composed in the time of the said

John Wyclif or since, or to be composed in the future, be read in part or in whole ... until the translation shall have been approved by the diocesan of the place'. In 1458 the statutes of King's and Queen's Colleges, Cambridge, were modified to require an oath against the heresies of Wyclif and Pecock, and in 1476 the University of Oxford assured the king that a search for Pecock's and Wyclif's books had been made and that a few had been burnt. As late as 1523 Bishop Tunstall of London wrote of the current unorthodox tendencies: 'It is no question of pernicious novelty; it is only that new arms are being added to the great crowd of Wycliffite heresies'.[14]

Throughout the fifteenth century vernacular access to the Bible story was therefore indirect, through devotional works such as Walter Hilton's *Scale of Perfection* or the popular *Mirror of the Life of Christ*, by Nicholas Love, prior of the Charterhouse of Mount Grace. This was presented to Archbishop Arundel in 1410, and became an important part of his riposte to Lollardy, as a substitute for a true translation. It is full of warm and memorable passages which make its popularity in English still easy to appreciate; its devotional and instructional temper may be gathered from a passage on the Annunciation:

> And so anon, Gabriel rising up, glad and jocund, took his flight from the high heavens down to earth, and in a moment he was, in man's likeness, before the virgin Mary. She was at that time closeted in her privy chamber at her prayers, or in her meditations, peradventure reading the prophecy of Isaiah touching the incarnation. And yet, so swiftly as he flew, his Lord was come before him, and there he found all the Holy Trinity come before their messenger. For thou shalt understand that this blessed incarnation was the high work of all the holy Trinity, though it so be that alone the person of the Son was incarnate and became man. (Part 1, chapter 3; the spelling has been modernised)

The dearth of a real translation of the Bible was justified by the convention of maintaining that English was not yet a suitable vehicle for translation of the Bible, that English was not yet considered a literary language; as a prose medium it was still characterised as 'rude' and 'barbarous'. Sir Thomas Elyot in 1531 in the preface to *The Boke named the Governour* complains of the difficulty made by the poverty of the language. He in fact invented in that book such terms as 'modesty', 'mediocrity', 'industrious', 'frugality', 'beneficence', but the complaint has all the marks of a literary convention. It is possible to quote contemporary casual figures about illiteracy, but it is important to remember that these testimonies are suspect because their authors have an axe to grind. Thus Thomas More in his *Apology* (1523) is arguing directly that there is no point in translating the Bible into English when he makes the estimate that 'people far more than four parts of all the whole divided into ten could never read english yet, and many now too old to go to school'.

A quarter of a century later Bishop Stephen Gardiner of Winchester's estimate is still more pessimistic when he writes (*Letter*, May 1547) that 'not one in a hundredth part of the realm' could read. These are not serious estimates, let alone reliable statistics, and evidence to the contrary may be garnered from the numerous heresy trials where possession and use of heretical books forms a regular part of the accusation, even among the artisan classes. This is not to deny that Latin remained the language of scholarship for at least another century. As late as 1605 of the 60,000 volumes listed in the *First Printed Catalogue of the Bodleian Library* (facsimile edition, 1986) only 60 are in English. There were, however, plenty of good plain works, manuals of instruction on medicine, hawking, cooking, behaviour. There were letters, such as the Paston and Stonor letters, which are often playful and merry. There was the English Chronicle, which Tyndale claims to have read as a child (*The Obedience of a Christian Man*, preface), and which may well have had no small influence on his purposeful, episodic style. John Dorne, however, the bookseller of Oxford, also records the sale in 1520 of several copies of a Latin book on dining-room etiquette, named *Stans puer ad Mensam* – the first half of a hexameter; was it entirely in Latin verse? It is also significant that in that year Dorne also sold several copies of Luther's *De Potestate Papae* at 3d each. One in every seven customers bought a work by Erasmus,[15] of whom we shall soon hear more.

Gutenberg and the Invention of Printing

Before any discussion of Tyndale's own achievement something must be said about the invention which changed the whole context of book-production, possibly the greatest ever revolution in information technology. Books and reading are, of course, correlative: as the art of reading becomes more widespread, so must books; as books become more widespread, so does reading. The mass-production of books was proceeding apace in the fifteenth century. There were guilds of copyists in the university city of Paris. At the height of the Renaissance in Florence Vespasiano da Bisticci employed fifty scribes. It fell, however, to a goldsmith to develop the most revolutionary response to the need for books. To do this Johann Gutenberg needed to overcome several diverse problems.

Block-printing was no novelty; it was practised widely in the first third of the fifteenth century. This consisted of carving onto a single wooden block both picture and some text, which was then inked and impressed onto paper.[16] This was suitable only for very short publications, for it was laborious, cumbersome and lacked flexibility. Gutenberg's invention was movable type, which could be combined in different patterns and re-used. He worked in the strictest secrecy, so that we can no longer recover the genesis of his ideas, but it is tempting to believe that his first inspiration was the hallmark, an individual punch still used by goldsmiths and silversmiths to show the manufacturer and date of any gold or silver product. In England such hallmarks had been in existence since at least 1300. Since then all silver objects made in London are stamped with a lion's head; in 1363 marks of individual makers were added. These individual punches of a single letter or symbol could be replicated in a mould, equipped with a shank which would enable them to be fitted together and combined in different patterns to make words.

There were other problems.

- The printing-press made use of a screwed metal press of the type used for squeezing olives for oil or grapes for wine. It was already used in the manufacture of paper, for squeezing the water out of the paper. The difficulty here was smudging, which Gutenberg overcame by evolving a box, called a 'hose', to hold the press steady.

● Perhaps the greatest difficulty was to find a quick-drying ink. For writing onto vellum (or parchment) a water-based ink had been used. This was unsuitable, both because it remained on the surface of the material, and so could be scraped off, and because it dried too slowly for the production of multiple copies. Gutenberg therefore developed the use of an ink based on lampblack (or soot) and varnish, which sank into the paper (made from rag and fibre), dried quickly without smudging and remained permanent.

The evolution of these processes was not completed in a day. The process of invention was long, and had to be shrouded in the strictest secrecy. There was no law of patent in those days, and Gutenberg clearly dreaded his burgeoning ideas being pirated. So much is clear from the evidence in a lawsuit brought against him by the heirs of one of his partners who died unexpectedly in 1438. The heirs were sworn to secrecy, but there is talk of Gutenberg presiding over the destruction of metal 'forms' just before the partner's death, and one witness testified that the partner had hoped to recover within a year the large capital (500 guilders) he had invested in the project. Another witness, a goldsmith, attests that in 1436 he had received from Gutenberg 100 guilders for printing-materials.[17] This was only the beginning of Gutenberg's troubles, for the expensive development-process was to run for another 20 years yet.

In 1448 Gutenberg borrowed from Johann Fust, a lawyer of Mainz, the large sum of 800 guilders at 6 per cent, and in 1452 another 800. Three years later Fust foreclosed on the loan, was awarded the whole business by the courts, and carried it on with his son-in-law, Peter Schoeffer, who had been Gutenberg's foreman. Tragically, Gutenberg himself was – like many another successful inventor – reduced to poverty, and ended his life in 1468 as a pensioner of the archbishop of Mainz. We simply do not and cannot know the human factors which led to the unhappy expulsion of the inventor. Did Fust wait to pounce till lucrative success was assured or was he impatient at the long delays? In 1454 Gutenberg printed some *Indulgences*, using the same type as would subsequently be used for the Bible,[18] single sheets which might have been either prototype-experiments or attempts to recoup some of the money. Fust may have regarded them as a distraction.

The production of the first Bible must have been well advanced when Fust foreclosed. The first printed Bible, known either as the 42-line Bible (from the 42 lines per page) or the Mazarine Bible (from the ownership of one copy by Cardinal Mazarin) must have been at least near completion, for one of the 40 remaining copies bears a handwritten note that Heinrich Cremer, vicar of St Stephen's in Mainz, finished the rubrics and the binding on 24 August 1456. Nearly complete were two other great works, the 36-line Bible (which was published sometime between 1457 and 1461) and a fine Latin psalter, produced by Fust and Schoeffer, dated 14 August 1457.

From this beginning, Bible-printing spread rapidly, Germany producing some hundred editions of the Vulgate by the end of the century, Venice seventeen and France eight. England lagged far behind. One reason was that England was far less advanced in printing than the continent. Caxton learnt printing as late as 1471/2 in Cologne, and it was not until 1477 that he published at Westminster the first book to be printed in England. For contrast we may compare the printing of biblical translations on the continent. A German Bible was printed already in 1466, and before Caxton's first English book there were already Bibles printed in Italian (1471), French (1474) and Dutch (1477), to be closely followed by printed versions in Catalan (1478) and Czech (1488).

William Tyndale

Even if printing had been more advanced, in England there simply was as yet no vernacular Bible to print. The reaction to Wyclif's Bible had seen to that. The first English Bible was almost single-handedly the achievement of William Tyndale. Tyndale bestrides the English Bible as Jerome bestrides the Latin. The field is perhaps more restricted, for the English Bible does not touch the whole of western Christianity, but the dominance is similar. The reputation of each scholar touches the whole of the work, although neither translator worked on more than a major portion of the text, rather than the whole. The whole thrust of

Tyndale's approach is well illustrated by the famous story from Foxe's *Book of Martyrs*:

> 'Master Tyndale happened to be in the company of a certain divine, recounted for a learned man, and in communing and disputing with him he drave him to that issue, that the said great doctor burst out into these blasphemous words, and said: "We were better to be without God's laws than the pope's". Master Tyndale, hearing this, full of godly zeal and not bearing that blasphemous saying, replied again and said: "I defy the pope and all his laws", and further added that, if God spared him life, ere many years he would cause the boy that driveth the plough to know more of scripture than he did'.

Tyndale is the heir of both Wyclif and Erasmus. He is the heir of Wyclif in sharing Wyclif's impatience with ecclesiastical authority, and especially his estimation of the authority of the Bible as above ecclesiastical rulings. He echoes Wyclif in his complaint[19] that at Oxford study of the Bible was postponed till after several years of previous learning, 'Ye drive them [students] from God's word and will let no man come thereto until he have been two years master of arts'.[20] His contempt for the methods of that study may be gathered from another comment: 'Of what text thou provest hell, another limbo patrum and another the assumption of our lady, and another shall prove of the same that an ape hath a tail.' His basic complaint is that this is putting the cart before the horse, or as he put it, measuring the meteyard [tape-measure] by the cloth.

As for Erasmus, Tyndale's mention of the ploughboy must surely be a reminiscence of Erasmus' preface to his 1516 first printed edition of the Greek New Testament: 'I could wish that all women should read the Gospel and St Paul's Epistles. I wish the farm worker might sing parts of them at the plough and the weaver might hum them at the shuttle, and the traveller might beguile the weariness of the way by reciting them'. Erasmus was by this time the most famous of all the humanists and – to judge from John Dorne's book-lists (see page 71) – the guru of every young scholar. He had visited Oxford in 1499 and been captivated by John Colet's[21] lectures on the Epistle to the Romans; he writes

to Colet, calling him 'praeceptor optime', 'unice praeceptor'
(*Letters* 225, 227). Colet was still lecturing on the Latin text, but
it was these lectures, on top of his admiration for Jerome, which
inspired Erasmus to learn Greek. Erasmus sprang into European
prominence in 1500 with the publication of the first of many
editions of his *Adagia*, a sort of commonplace book: 'there was
probably no other work from Erasmus' hand which had a greater
impact on European culture than this'.[22] To take a couple of small
instances, it was from Erasmus' *Adagia* that the practices of washing cups and sheets between use by different persons became
widespread. In 1511, when Tyndale was a finalist undergraduate
at Oxford, Erasmus was back in Cambridge, complaining about
the poor quality of the food and drink, and lecturing on Jerome,
for Jerome had long been Erasmus' own great hero and master. In
his early twenties he writes, 'Not only had I read them, but,
despite their number, copied them out' (Letter 22). Erasmus was
moved by the piety of this 'unworldly man, incontrovertibly far
the most learned and eloquent of all Christians' (Letter 141). A
major boost was given to biblical translation by his publication
of the Greek New Testament. The biblical text itself is quite
inferior, hurried and slipshod work. Erasmus was working from
only seven twelfth-century manuscripts of the 'Byzantine' text-
type, the type approved by the Greek Orthodox Church for liturgical use. Erasmus never intended it as a critical edition, merely as
a support for his own *Adnotationes*. Where the manuscripts
differed, he simply adopted the majority view, a solution quick
and simple but utterly at odds with any principles of modern
textual criticism, which enters into a complicated and delicate discussion of the worth of a manuscript reading. In the year before
publication Erasmus writes to Reuchlin that he has finished his
Adnotationes, 'and so have in mind to print the New Testament in
Greek with my comments added'.

Theologically important, in the climate of renewal which was
beginning to breed the Reformation, was also the parallel new
Latin translation which Erasmus provided. Translation itself
can be persuasive. At Matthew 3:2 John the Baptist proclaims
μετανοεῖτε (μετανοία). The Hebrew/Aramaic word which
stands behind this means 'to turn back, go in a different direction'. The Baptist is exhorting to a total change of life and
priorities. Jerome's Latin translation, *poenitentiam agite*, had

become one of the bases for the multiple acts of penance practised in the medieval Church in order to make atonement for sin, a quite different concept. Erasmus' translation, *resipiscite*, 'become wise again, come to your senses', distances itself from this medieval preoccupation. Similarly the Vulgate translation of the angel's greeting to Mary, *Ave, gratia plena*, gave rise to the idea of a vessel full of grace, and so to the notion of piling up merits. Erasmus' *gratiosa* for the Greek κεχαριτομένη avoids this implication and is closer to the biblical idea of the loving and unmerited favour of God for Mary.[23]

A second edition was made within three years, and three thousand copies were sold of these first two editions. It formed the basis also of Luther's translation into German, and, later, of the King James Version.

Not long after Tyndale's conversation with the 'certain divine' in rural Gloucestershire, where Tyndale was tutor to the children of Sir John Walsh, came the decisive move to break the jinx on translations of the Bible into English. Tyndale offered himself in 1520 as a translator to that noted humanist and friend of Erasmus, Cuthbert Tunstall, bishop of London. It is striking that as his sample submission to Tunstall Tyndale chose so luxuriantly and artificial a rhetorical author as Isocrates. He had, however, clearly already given thought to the requirements of biblical translation. In *The Obedience of a Christian Man* he writes:

> The Greek tongue agreeth a thousand times more with the English than with the Latin. The manner of speaking is both one, so that in a thousand places thou needest not but to translate it into the English word for word, when thou must seek a compass in the Latin, and yet shall have much work to translate it well favouredly, so that it have the same grace and sweetness, sense and pure understanding with it in the Latin, and as it hath in the Hebrew. A thousand parts better may it be translated into the English than into the Latin.

Tyndale was quite right about the similarity of English to Greek and the dissimilarity of both to Latin, for Latin is a square and chunky language, whereas English and Greek are flexible and agile. Tunstall, however, refused his request, on the grounds that he had no room for him in his household. The subsequent history makes it quite clear that Tunstall was a dedicated opponent of Bible translation. Having been cold-shouldered by Tunstall, Tyndale went abroad to Flanders in April 1524, to pursue his objectives in the more tolerant air of the continent. He first set about translating the New Testament, and by the summer of 1525 he had got as far as printing the middle of Matthew chapter 22 at Cologne, when the authorities set out to arrest him. However, he fled to Worms, where he finished and published the New Testament, complete with copious notes which were heavily indebted to Luther.

Tyndale's Translation

As soon as this translation began arriving in England Tunstall mounted a virulent campaign against it. On the physical level he had the books burnt as they arrived at the docks. Finding this to be insufficiently effective, he arranged that his agent Packyngton should buy up Tyndale's entire stock, thus effectively clearing Tyndale's considerable debt, 'so the bishop had the books, Packyngton the thanks and Tyndale had the money'.[24] On the intellectual level Tunstall commissioned Thomas More, one of the greatest of Renaissance scholars and soon to become Lord Chancellor, to attack the translation. More's violent, not to say scatological, attack pilloried it as 'Luther's Testament'. Linguistically, the translation was of course indebted to Luther, though certainly independent, and in places correcting Luther, for Tyndale was a better Greek scholar than Luther (even though Luther had help from Melanchthon). Similarly later, in his Old Testament translation, Tyndale clearly had correct and alert access to the Hebrew text. He obviously consulted Luther's translation, but differs from Luther sufficiently often to leave no doubt that he made his own judgement about the meaning of the Hebrew and the best way of rendering it. Theologically, however, the Lutheran tendencies protrude even in the translation. More's attack focussed on three translation options in which Tyndale, exercising his Lollard or Lutheran legacy, had deliberately set about avoiding the overtones of ecclesiastical tradition. For the traditional 'priest' Tyndale used 'senior' or 'elder', for 'church' he used 'congregation' and for 'charity' he used 'love' – all thoroughly defensible but theologically explosive options. Tyndale obviously wanted to avoid 'churchy' language; More wanted to retain it.

Uncowed, Tyndale set about translating the Old Testament. His Pentateuch was published in 1530 in five distinct books, probably to make it more portable, and the book of Jonah in 1531. On experimenting, I found that a 1534 copy of Tyndale's *Genesis* fitted comfortably into the back pocket of my trousers – convenient to carry around. At his death Tyndale also left a translation of Joshua to Chronicles which was later used in the Matthew's Bible (see p. 87). However, in 1536 he was, at the instigation of the English authorities, kidnapped in Vilvorde, incarcerated and eventually garrotted, his body being burnt at the same stake. His undaunted spirit and his continuing passion for language and translation is shown in his letter to the prison governor:

> I suffer greatly from cold in the head and am afflicted with perpetual catarrh. I ask to have a lamp in the evening; it is indeed wearisome sitting alone in the dark. Most of all I beg and beseech Your Clemency to urge the Commissary that he will kindly permit me to have the Hebrew Bible, Hebrew grammar and Hebrew dictionary, that I may pass the time in that study.

The Genius of Tyndale

Two elements combine to make Tyndale's translation the fascinating work it is. The first is Tyndale's extraordinary grasp of language and his determination to make the text both readable and intelligible, the second his knowledge and use of Hebrew. The brilliance of Tyndale as a translator has never been surpassed. By comparison to the earlier, Wycliffite, version it wins through always by its rhythm and balance. Basic as it was to the King James Version, the later translators sometimes felt obliged to moderate its boldness, perhaps improving the accuracy but in the process losing some of the sparkle. Three examples of this genius may be given.

1. Tyndale's eight Beatitudes by comparison to the Wycliffite version. Some significant changes are italicised in the earlier version.

Wyclif:

Blessed ben poor *men* in spirit, for the kingdom of heaven is herne.

Blessed ben mild *men*, for they schulen welde the earth.

Blessed ben they that mournen, for they schulen be comforted.

Blessed ben they that hungren and thristen righteousness, for they schulen be *fulfilled*.

Blessed ben merciful *men*, for they schulen *get* mercy.

Blessed ben *they that be of* clean heart, for they schulen see God.

Blessed ben peacable *men*, for they schulen be cleppid Goddis children.

Blessed ben they that suffren persecution for rightfulness, for the kingdom of heaven is herne.

Tyndale:

Blessed are the poor in spirit, for theirs is the kingdom of heaven.

Blessed are they that mourn, for they shall be comforted.

Blessed are the meek, for they shall inherit the earth.

Blessed are they which hunger and thirst for righteousness, for they shall be filled.

Blessed are the merciful, for they shall obtain mercy.

Blessed are the pure in heart, for they shall see God.

Blessed are the maintainers of peace, for they shall be called the children of God.

Blessed are they which suffer persecution for righteousness' sake, for theirs is the kingdom of heaven.

2.   A direct and succinct style:

Tyndale: 'Break no wedlock, kill not, steal not.' (Matthew 19:18)

King James: 'Thou shalt do not murder, thou shalt not commit adultery, thou shalt not steal.'

Tyndale: 'whoever asketh receiveth' (Matthew 7:8)

King James: 'everyone that asketh receiveth'.

3.   Verve and wit:

Genesis 3:4: 'Tush, ye shall not die' (KJV 'Ye shall not surely die').

Matthew 15:22: 'My daughter is piteously (KJV 'grievously') vexed with a devil'.

Matthew 15:26: 'It is not good to take the children's bread and cast it to whelps (KJV 'dogs').

Matthew 16:8: 'Why are your minds cumbered (KJV 'why

reason ye among yourselves') because ye have brought no bread?'

In any case, Tyndale's achievement is sufficiently proved by the fact that his translation has formed the basis of every subsequent English version. In the King James Version some 80 per cent of those books which Tyndale translated has been adopted word for word. The number of phrases which have become proverbial and unnoticed current coin in the English language is countless ('the powers that be', 'the fat of the land', 'not unto us, O Lord, not unto us'), the number of words felicitously invented by Tyndale is remarkable ('passover', 'long-suffering', 'scapegoat'). Three qualities which show his genius as a translator are rhythm, direct-ness and a witty gaiety ('Tush, ye shall not die', says the tempting serpent to the woman). Changes made by subsequent versions may improve on details of accuracy and steadiness (particularly in restraining Tyndale's passion for *variatio*), but always, even in the case of the King James Version, at the cost of vigour and boldness. It has been calculated that by the time of Tyndale's death in 1536, perhaps 16,000 copies of his translation had been brought into England, a country with a population at that time of some two and a half million.[25]

FIVE

The King James Bible

The English Bible in the Later Sixteenth Century

In an age in which Bible-reading is primarily a private activity by which the reader seeks to foster personal devotion to God and to come to know better the ways of God it is difficult to appreciate the public and political passions aroused by particular versions of the Bible. In the sixteenth century books were still rare enough for the Bible to have a position of unrivalled prominence in home and church, and above all in the minds and thoughts of individuals. Preference for a particular version of the Bible constituted a much stronger statement of position than any modern statement expressed by preference for newspaper, television programme, football team or style of music.

During the reign of Henry VIII the story of the different Bible versions is intimately linked with that monarch's passionate and difficult task of both drawing the people with him and achieving uniformity and peace in religion.[1] Henry was no reformer. He wanted only independence from Rome, whose authorities had refused to legitimize his divorce, and whose interference limited his autocratic rule. In matters of doctrine he remained orthodox, conservative and determined to retain control of religious developments. Although his early *Assertio Septem Sacramentorum* (1521) received substantial help from Thomas More, he retained enough personal interest in theology to argue extensively about the interpretation of Origen in a letter to Tunstall late in his reign. In any case, reform or no reform, Henry's break from Rome and nationalisation of the English Church implied also a break from the Latin Vulgate and so an English Bible.

The three principal sponsored Bible versions which resulted during Henry VIII's reign were all secondary to other translations. Each constituted an attempt by the sponsoring authority to form the minds and hearts of the people. Their principal interest is therefore not the translation but the politico-religious situation which they illustrate. Henry recognised that the English Church required an English Bible, and that this was desired by many – the

Convocation of Canterbury petitioned the king as early as 1534 that 'the whole Bible might be translated into English'. Coverdale's Bible was dedicated to the king, and its title-page shows the king delivering the Bible to his bishops, but the king insisted that the reading of the Bible be strictly controlled. He did indeed order that a Bible should be placed in every parish church, but this did not imply free access to all, still less freedom of interpretation. Accordingly an Act of 1543 forbade the reading of the Bible by women (except noblewomen), merchants, artificers, journeymen, yeomen and labourers. In his last address to parliament he warned against the use of the Bible 'to dispute and make scripture a railing and taunting stock against priests and preachers. I am very sorry to know and hear how irreverently that most precious jewel the word of God is disputed, rimed, sung and jangled in every ale-house and tavern'.[2]

Coverdale's Bible (1535) – a complete English Bible

Of the three Bibles which were produced during the reign of Henry VIII the first was Miles Coverdale's. It was not authorized by, but was dedicated to the king (who appears on the title page, enthroned and handing the volume to the mitred bishops). It was the first complete Bible to be printed in English, and printed in Zurich! However, apart from Coverdale's melodious rendering of the Psalms, which has become beloved by its adoption into the Book of Common Prayer, it is not in itself an important version, though J.F. Mozley maintains that 'in the line of scholars who made our King James' bible the name of Coverdale stands second only to Tyndale'.[3] Coverdale had no pretensions to being an original scholar. He was ignorant of both Greek and Hebrew, translating from the Latin, and admitting in his preface that he relied on five interpreters: these have been discerned as the Vulgate; Pagnini's Latin of 1528 (a meticulously mechanical translation of the Hebrew, retaining even the Hebrew spelling of names, e.g. 'Somron' for Samaria, 'Selomoh' for Solomon); Luther's German (from which Coverdale derived such monster forms as 'overbodycoat' Exodus 25:7 for Luther's 'leibrock',[4] 'morningshine' Isaiah 59:9, and 'winesupper' for Luther's 'weinseuffer' Joel 1:5 which in modern English would be 'wine-bibber'); the Zürich Bible of 1531; and Tyndale (using the revised version of the Pentateuch and the New Testament, but not including his Joshua to Chronicles).

Matthew's Bible (1537) – an annotated Bible

Coverdale was closely followed by the so-called 'Matthew's Bible' (1537); this was in fact the work not of Thomas Matthew, but of John Rogers. Cranmer, the archbishop of Canterbury, had long before attempted to enlist the help of his bishops in authorizing a translation, but had met only opposition, at any rate from the bishop of London.[5] He now recognized that the bishops would not authorize a translation 'till a day after domesday' and submitted this version to the king. The fact that it was not a bare text but had some 2,000 notes will have pleased the king, though the content of the notes less, since many of them were by Luther, Tyndale and other Reformers. The translation drew heavily on Tyndale (including the first publication of his Joshua to Chronicles) and lightly on Coverdale.

The Great Bible (1541) – a parish Bible

In 1538 Thomas Cromwell, the king's vicar general, reiterated to the bishops the royal wish that a Bible in English be 'openly laid forth in every parish church at the charges and costs of the parson and vicars'. For this purpose Cranmer found neither of the two previous publications satisfactory: the text of Coverdale was insufficiently authentic and the notes of Matthew too inflammatory. Accordingly he entrusted to Coverdale the task of editing a third Bible, which from its parish-lectern size (38cm x 23cm) became known as 'The Great Bible'. Again, the importance of the royal patronage and control is shown by the title-page woodcut of Henry handing the Bible to Cromwell and Cranmer, amid cheering populace – and 'Vivat Rex' inscribed on the pulpit. The conservative temper of the time is shown by the respect paid to Latin and to the Vulgate. The version is founded on Matthew's Bible, but the Old Testament corrected according to Münster's Hebrew-Latin diglot edition of 1535 and the New Testament according to Erasmus' Latin version. One important conservative element is that the four books of the New Testament which Luther considered suspect (Hebrew, James, Jude and Revelation) are printed according to their place in the Vulgate, rather than in a separate category at the end. This ordering was followed by the King James

Version, and so remained standard in English Bibles. Where the Vulgate differs from these, its version is included – for the sake of the firm conservatives – in small type. A set of endnotes was planned, and the hand-symbol Λ inserted in the text at appropriate places, but no notes (apart from minimal marginal cross-references) were ever included; was the task of composing them too delicate, or was the revision simply too rushed? This Bible, the first to be widely available, proved hugely popular, despite its price of 12 shillings bound (a labourer's wage for two weeks): an estimated 20,000 copies were printed by 1541,[6] and the crowds who gathered round to read the six copies placed in St Paul's Cathedral were so noisy that the bishop of London had to forbid such reading during the service.

The Geneva Bible (1560) – a study-Bible for Protestants

Apart from these versions presented to the English people under royal patronage, two sixteenth-century translations deserve mention, the Geneva Bible and the Rheims-Douai version. The Geneva Bible was the child of Protestant exiles in Calvin's Geneva, under the leadership of William Whittingham, a Marian exile who returned under Elizabeth to become dean of Durham in 1563. It was a sort of study-Bible equipped with illustrations and with copious maps, tables and notes, the notes being heavily dependent on Calvin himself and his theological orientation.[7] This was the first English Bible to be printed in Roman type, rather than the cumbersome and archaic 'black letter' type. It was also the first to have divisions into chapters and verses, thus making both reading and reference incomparably easier. The text was scholarly and thoughtful, a thorough and responsible revision of the Great Bible in the light of the important scholarship of the previous half-century. It was the first Bible to be printed in Scotland. In England it was given a cautious royal licence, subject to the approval of the bishops of Canterbury and London. While the Great Bible remained the official version for parish churches, it was the Geneva Bible, with its Calvinistic notes, which was the popular Bible throughout Elizabeth's reign. The popularity of the Geneva Bible is easy to understand. With its helpful apparatus, illustrations and maps, it is attractive and easy to use even today. For the Bible-reading conventicles for which it was intended (and in which it was copiously used) some sort of notes are essential. It was printed in every size: folio, quarto, octavo, duodecimo and even sextodecimo.

The Bishops' Bible (1569) – an unsuccessful compromise

Before long, however, the Calvinistic tone of the apparatus was seen to threaten the delicate balance of retention and reform which Queen Elizabeth and her ministers were intent on forging in the Church of England. In 1566 Archbishop Parker instructed a new team, mostly bishops, to prepare a new version, removing the 'bitter notes'. This compromise version, 'the Bishops' Bible' was ready in three years, but it never won the enthusiastic success enjoyed by the Geneva Bible. As a whole its production is a throwback from the Geneva Bible, making it far less attractive to handle and to use. In addition, Parker's Protestant successor as archbishop, Grindal, encouraged the use of the Geneva Bible, and during his archiepiscopate there were no editions of the Bishops' Bible. In the years 1583–1603 there were 51 editions of the former as against only 7 of the latter. The Geneva Bible is the version principally used by Shakespeare, and is even the text quoted (14 times) in the preface to the King James Bible.

The Rheims-Douai Version (1582/1609) – a Bible for Catholics

Another group of exiles also produced their Bible. Cardinal William Allen set up a college at Rheims for the education of Catholic clergy, who would later return to the English Mission, working for the return of England to the traditional Catholic faith and practice. It was felt essential that they should have their own English version of the Bible to counter the Protestant Bibles now available, as is explained frankly in the preface. This version was prepared by the Oxford scholar and teacher at Rheims, Gregory Martin, with the help of Richard Bristow. It was based primarily on the Vulgate, which had been declared the official Bible of the Church at the Council of Trent in 1546, though marginal notes also refer to the Greek. The translation is marked by the deliberate retention of latinisms, sometimes to bizarre effect, such as 'our supersubstantial bread' in the Lord's Prayer (Matthew 6:11), or 'every knee shall bow, of celestials, terrestrials and infernals' (Philippians 2:10). This literal fidelity to the Vulgate sometimes produced meaningless phrases, e.g. 'A vineyard was made to my beloved in horn, the son of oil' (Isaiah 5:1). This extraordinary gobbledegook goes back, through the LXX, to the Hebrew. In Hebrew the same word is used for an animal's horn and (derivatively) for an isolated hill. 'Son of' often means 'the product of', so 'son of oil' or 'son of fat' means 'rich, fertile'. Hence the modern translation, 'My beloved had a vineyard on a fertile hillside'.

Particularly vulnerable in the Douai Version were the Psalms, where the translation was based on Jerome's Gallican Psalter, whose reverence for the Hebraisms mirrored already in the Septuagint had often produced an unintelligible rendering. The Bible was copiously equipped with notes, naturally concentrating especially on specifically Catholic doctrines, such as the virgin birth (Matthew 1:25) and the Petrine primacy (Matthew 16:18). The New Testament appeared in 1582 and the Old Testament – after the transfer of the College to Douai – in 1609/10. This Rheims-Douai version (in a 1772 revision by Bishop Richard Challoner) remained the Bible of English Catholics until well into the twentieth century.

The King James Bible

The Genesis of the Version

King James VI of Scotland came to the throne of England as James I with the determination of reconciling the Puritan tendencies he knew too well from Scotland with the traditionalism of the Church of England. He was a strangely unprepossessing person, who never knew his parents and was crowned king of Scotland when only one year old. When he was 18 the French ambassador wrote of him:

> He is learned in many languages and has a marvellous mind. His manners are aggressive and very uncouth, in speaking, eating, clothing, games and conversation in the company of women. His carriage is ungainly, his steps erratic.[8]

His upbringing as king among Puritans had produced in him by reaction a fierce belief in the divine right of kings. His view of the monarchy is well reflected by his statement:

As the king is overlord of the whole land, so is he master over every person that inhabiteth the same, having power over the life and death of every one of them. For although a just prince will not take the life of any of his subjects without a clear law, yet the same laws whereby he taketh them are made by himself or his predecessors, and so the power flows always from himself (*Workes*, p. 202).

He could quote scripture in his support, as in the speech to Parliament on 21 March 1610: 'Kings are not only God's lieutenants upon earth and sit upon God's throne, but even by God himself they are called gods' (alluding to Psalm 82:6). He would not therefore be sympathetic to the Geneva Bible which held popular sway in England. Its annotations are decidedly critical of monarchs, often using the word 'tyrants' (a word significantly never used in the King James Version), praising Daniel for disobeying 'the king's wicked commandment', for a king 'ought to do nothing by which God would be dishonoured'. Furthermore, the note to Psalm 105:15 applies the expression 'mine anointed' to the people of God, when King James would certainly consider it to refer to the king himself. James left no doubt in *Basilikon Doron*, written as guidance to his son and would-be successor, that the right of kings is God-given and that this can be proved by the scriptures.

Already on his way south to England from Scotland James was approached by the Puritans, who expected him to be sympathetic to their cause, and presented him with the Millenniary Petition (signed by a thousand people), detailing their grievances. To address these grievances he summoned a conference in Hampton Court the year after his accession. In fact at this conference he made fun of the Puritans in a most unregal way. However, speaking on behalf of the Puritans, the Reformed Protestant president of Corpus Christi College, Oxford, John Rainolds, suggested a new translation of the Bible, and the method by which it should be done: six panels of translators, two at Oxford, Cambridge and Westminster respectively, each charged with a set section of the Bible. This should be submitted for revision and approval in turn to the bishops, the royal Privy Council and the king himself. The king seems to have jumped at this idea, for the most widespread of the current Bibles was the Geneva Bible, which he considered 'the worst' of all. He said he found the notes 'very partiell, untrue, seditious and savouring too much of daungerous and trayterous conceits'. The notes were indeed not favourable to kingship. In his zeal to replace the Geneva Bible and its notes he was perfectly right. In fact he had already suggested a revision of the Geneva Bible to the Kirk Assembly in Scotland in 1601. As Bibles were now commonly available in translation, by the end of the sixteenth century 'the Bible was the source of virtually all ideas; it supplied the idiom in which men and women discussed them'.[9] It was the source not only for geology, astronomy and medicine, but also for heady political discussion. In a world before the invention of the distractions of the novel, the film and the television the Bible was so well known that subversive ideas could be expressed vividly by allusion. The Puritan notes to the Geneva Bible gave a consistent and powerful impetus to such subversion.

However, keeping rigorously to the principle of compromise, the king did not demand notes to set things right, but insisted that any new translation should merely be devoid of notes. Rules for translators were firmly laid down. The new Bible should follow the Bishops' Bible as closely as possible, avoiding some recent idiosyncracies like Hebraizing the spelling of names. The Bishops' Bible had spelt the son of Abraham as 'Izhàc' and the Geneva Bible as 'Isahac'. One instance of fidelity to the Bishops' Bible has had immense consequences for all ecclesiastical and biblical language in England, namely the retention of the second person singular, 'thou' and 'thee', which have been regularly used in hymns and prayers until very recently. There is strong evidence that this usage was waning (the court records of Durham in 1575 show that the singular was now being used only rather aggressively to social inferiors[10]). The translation–decision taken here may well have influenced the arrested development of the language on this point, so that the usage still continues in the north of England.

The new translation was to draw on the best of previous translations, mentioned in the careful instructions being Tyndale, Matthew's Bible, Coverdale, the Geneva Bible. In fact in at least one place (Hebrew 11:1) the Rheims–Douai version was also pillaged. Not only words but principles were invoked, for example, there was to be no attempt to standardize translation of one Greek word by the same English word. This imparts a certain liveliness but has disadvantages; thus in Romans 5:2–11 καύχωμαι is translated by three different words within nine verses. Similarly, since the panels worked independently of one another, quotations of the Old Testament in the New often differ from the version in their original position (e.g. Luke 3:4, 5).

Too strong a Puritan bias was to be avoided, in that the familiar traditional forms of words were to be retained rather than the Puritan equivalents, so 'church' not 'congregation', 'baptism' not 'washing'. Even-handedly, however, the final preface was written jointly by the Puritan sympathizer Miles Smith and the learned High Church bishop Thomas Bilson.

One important decision taken was to include the Apocrypha – surprisingly. Article Six of the 39 Articles of 1562 had reverted to the middle position taken by Origen and Jerome, neither fully accepting nor rejecting the apocryphal books: 'and the other books (as Hierome saith) the Church doth read for example of life and instruction of manners, but yet doth it not apply them to establish any doctrine'. King James himself was sharper; he wrote in *Basilikon Doron*, 'as to the Apocriphe bookes, I omit them because I am no Papist'. Similarly the Apocrypha are summarily dismissed a few years later by the Puritan Westminster Confession of Faith in 1646: 'The books commonly called Apocrypha, not being of divine inspiration, are no part of the Canon of Scripture, and therefore are of no authority in the Church of God, nor to be otherwise approved or made use of than other human writings.'

Although this version has frequently been termed 'the Authorized Version' there is in fact no record that when it appeared it had ever been finally authorized either by king or parliament or bishops. The title-page carries the note: 'appointed to be read in churches'. It is perhaps best called the 'King James Version', after the king who is so lavishly and unrealistically praised in its preface as 'the principle mover and author of the work'.

The Impact of the King James Version
Within a generation this version had superseded all others, though Roman Catholics clung tenaciously to the Rheims-Douai version. The King James Version was, of course, much cheaper to produce than the Geneva Bible, with its notes, tables and illustrations. In the Fast Sermons (i.e. sermons preached before

parliament on days of fasting) during the 1640s it was already this Bible which supplied the texts for penetrating political satire and persuasion. In the closing years of the reign of Charles I and at his trial in 1649, he was powerfully excoriated as 'the man of blood' (Numbers 35:33 in the King James Version), whose blood-guilt was defiling the land. In that Bible-dominated age, and throughout the Puritan revolution, the opportunities for making political capital by biblical symbol and allusion were endless.

It has retained this dominant position even to this day, despite the subsequent advance of language and of scholarship. Partly unintelligible to modern ears though it may be, the nobility and dignity of the language ensures that it is still read on formal and traditional occasions. The reading of 1 Corinthians 13 by the prime minister at the funeral of Diana, Princess of Wales was memorable. On the other hand there are passages where the archaic language can hardly fail to raise a smile even from a sympathetic modern listener. Jeremiah sees two baskets of figs, one with very good figs and the other with 'very naughty figs' (Jeremiah 24:2). Paul, asking Philemon to put new heart into him, writes, 'Refresh my bowels in the Lord' (Philemon 20). The psalmist, speaking of the reassurance God gives in sleep, sings, 'My reins also instruct me in the night seasons' (Psalm 16:7). But it is unfair to laugh at the elderly.

Perhaps the most serious limitation of the KJV is the Greek text from which it is derived, Erasmus' very mediocre Greek text. This text has now been thoroughly superseded through the wider availability and more careful evaluation of manuscripts since the sixteenth century, especially the revaluation of the three great manuscripts Vaticanus, Alexandrinus and Sinaiticus. Already at that time, however, the progress in Greek and Hebrew scholarship in nearly a century since Tyndale's version had prepared a much more solid basis for translation.

The climate was right for a great translation. During the years in which this version was being created an astonishing constellation of great writers was at work. Poets like John Donne (1572–1631), dramatists like William Shakespeare (1564–1616) and Ben Jonson (1573–1637), essayists like Francis Bacon (1561–1626), homilists like Launcelot Andrewes (1555–1626) were at the height of their powers, writing with vigour, drama and confidence. There was also a vigorous tradition behind it, stretching back uninterruptedly to Tyndale. The preface freely grants that 'we, building upon their foundation that went before us, and being holpen by their labours, do endeavour to make better that which they left us so good', and indeed it has been estimated that in 80 per cent of those books which Tyndale translated his version is retained. Departures from it are often less bold and imaginative, though perhaps more sober. Tyndale was a young and bold translator, deliberately setting out to reproduce the cragginess of the Hebrew. The King James Version is more polished, more rhetorical and even more baroque, sometimes reminiscent of the ornate style of the music and decorative visual arts of the period. The speech rhythms of the King James Version have entered into any elevated prose in the English language, and the expressions which have become proverbial, used by those who have no familiarity with the Bible and are quite unaware of their origin are numberless: 'sour grapes', 'go from strength to strength', 'the salt of the earth', 'a thorn in the flesh'.

The Bible taken by many of the English–speaking settlers when they crossed the Atlantic was the Geneva Bible, for many were Puritans, fleeing from religious intolerance in England. The King James Version gradually gained ground. The first Bible to be printed in North America was, however, in German in 1743. Throughout the British colonies Bibles without comment might be printed only by the Oxford and Cambridge University Presses (and one other licensed printer). This situation changed swiftly after Independence. In 1777 a group of three American clergymen petitioned Congress to give permission to print a Bible for the newly independent United States. It is significant that the request was refused simply on the grounds of lack of resources in print and paper. A New Testament was nevertheless printed in 1777, and in 1783 a whole Bible was produced with the approval of Congress by Robert Aitken, a Scottish publisher from Dalkeith, who had immigrated to Philadelphia in 1769. Although the title page claimed that the version was 'newly translated out of the original tongues', the only differences from the King James Version were the inclusion on the title page of this 'newly' and – not surprisingly – the omission of 'by his majesty's special command'!

The Missionary Movement

The whole situation of the dissemination of the Bible changed radically with the advent of the missionary movement of Christianity, first with the sixteenth-century Jesuit missions to the Far East, then with the opening up of North America and of the Indian subcontinent by the East India Companies, and finally with the discovery of Sub-Saharan Africa. On the whole the Bible has been an essential element in the missionary movement. There are perhaps two stages of this dissemination. The first is where the Bible is an instrument of preliminary evangelisation. There is no spreading Christianity without some version of the gospel, though there are still today regions (for example in northern Namibia) where ministers have to provide their own oral rendering, and others (for example the southern Philippines) where missionaries are still preparing a first written translation. The second phase is when Christianity has reached sufficient maturity for the indigenous speakers of a language to provide, or at least co-operate in providing, a lasting translation. The problems are made vastly greater than for translation into European languages by the need to move into another thought-world, far removed from the Mediterranean culture which is at the basis of western civilisation. Gestures, colours, climatic features, marriage-customs, images may carry entirely different overtones (the spirits have a different function in African religions from that of the Spirit in Judeo-Christian thought), though certain tribal or nomadic conditions in some areas may also make elements of the Old Testament world far more accessible than they are to modern western peoples. The oral culture which still prevails in many regions of Africa makes both the epic stories and the oral transmission of the earliest parts of the Bible readily intelligible and immediately attractive.

Catholic stress on the living tradition of teaching, and mistrust of the unsupervised reading of the Bible, meant that less priority was given to the provision of Bibles by Catholic than by Protestant missionaries. Remarkable among the early missions to the Far East were the Jesuit missions to China and Japan, for to them provision of a vernacular Bible was not a priority. Amid considerable production of books and of Christian literature, it simply does not seem to have occurred to them that a Bible should be included. In

1548 Francis Xavier, in his instructions for missioners in India, says plenty about reciting the Creed and the Articles of the Faith, about prayers and processions, but no word about the biblical text.[11] In 1604 the awesome polyglot Plantin edition of the Bible in eight volumes was brought to China in its own packing-case, but Matteo Ricci refused all requests to translate it, on the dubious grounds that special permission would be required from the pope.[12] It is striking that in 1590–1610 the Jesuit presses at Kyushu produced a whole series of catechetical and devotional books in Japanese, prayerbooks, *The Imitation of Christ*, lives of saints, the Exercises of St Ignatius and dictionaries. But neither a Bible nor even a New Testament is listed among the considerable number of books known to have been produced there,[13] though the Jesuits are said to have produced a complete New Testament (now lost) in Japanese in 1613. Similarly in Africa, though 'Protestant vernacular Bibles had multiplied across the continent before the close of the [19th] century, Catholic ones were simply non-existent'.[14]

Consequently it is to a Dutch Protestant, and a merchant in the Dutch East India Company, that falls the honour of the first known extended biblical translation into a non-European language: Albert Cornelius Ruyl translated the Gospel of Matthew into Malay in 1629. It was similarly a Dutch merchant, Bartholomaus Ziegelbalg, who was responsible for the first translation into Tamil in 1715. The first printed translation into a North American language was John Eliot's for the Mohican Indians of Massachussetts (1663).

The evangelical revival in England at the beginning of the nineteenth century was a particularly potent force for spreading the biblical text around the expanding British Empire. The Baptist missionary William Carey at Seranpur in 1800–1833 oversaw the translation of the Bible into Bengali, Maratha, Tamil and altogether 26 Indian languages. The most powerful manifestation of the evangelical movement, however, was the foundation of the Bible societies. The first of these, the British and Foreign Bible Society, was formed (1804) at a meeting at the London Tavern in Bishopsgate, strangely enough initially in response to a demand for Bibles in Welsh. The cry was raised that if this was possible in the British Isles, why not to the whole of the British Empire, indeed to the whole world? The society was deliberately lay and inter-denominational, with a committee consisting of 15 Anglican and 15 Free Church laymen, joined by six representatives of European Churches, and pledged to distribute Bibles 'without note or comment'. Within a decade Bible societies had been formed in Germany, Russia, Greece, the United States and many other countries, as independent offshoots of the parent society. These societies were instrumental in translating the Bible into the languages to which Christianity was spreading through the burgeoning missionary movement. Thus, to take only two examples, in 1806 Bibles in Spanish were taken to Buenos Aires 'probably for the first time in the history of South America'.[15] In 1812 Robert Morrison secured the post of interpreter to the East India Company and began the translation of the Bible into Chinese, in the hope that China would soon be opened to Christian missionaries.

This work was carried on with impressive zeal and perseverance. By the time of the Golden Jubilee of the British and Foreign Bible Society in 1854 it was reckoned that 28 million copies of scripture had been distributed in 152 languages and dialects. In 1997 the Bible Society (as it had been renamed) claimed translation of the whole Bible into 349 languages and dialects, and individual books into 2,123 languages. In 1995 they distributed 560 million Bibles or parts of Bibles. They reckoned that there still remained some 4,000 languages without any scripture.

SIX

Modern Versions of the Bible in English

The Revised Standard Version and New Revised Standard Version

It was only after the Second World War that a proliferation of new versions of the Bible into English occurred.[1] Several factors contributed to this explosion.

- The archaeological, literary and textual studies of the previous century had begun to trickle down beyond the merely academic world. Historical and educational programmes on radio and television stimulated an increasing interest in roots and origins.
- There was a renewed impetus in Christianity not only to expunge the shame felt at the atrocities of war but also to counter the opposition of secularism, atheism and Communism.
- Popular interest in the origins of Christianity was further aroused by sensationalist claims following the discovery in 1945 of the Nag Hammadi writings and in 1946 of the Dead Sea Scrolls (or, more accurately, the scrolls discovered in the Judaean Desert).
- The increase in both literacy and wealth was making books more available and common.
- From the point of view of English-language Bibles this was especially the case in the Third World, where English was becoming increasingly known and read, a more or less universal second language. Correspondingly, in Europe and America English was largely replacing French as the *lingua franca*. Among the many available, four versions will be profiled here.

The first of the new translations to appear was the Revised Standard Version, commissioned in 1937 and completed in 1952. Despite being the work of American scholars, and based on the American Standard Version (itself a revision, made in 1901, of the King James Version) it has become fully accepted on both sides of the Atlantic as a dignified and accurate translation, being widely used both in public reading and for academic work. A number of archaisms (such as 'saith') and semitisms (such as 'and it came to pass that') have been eliminated, and 'thou' was finally retained only for addressing God (not Jesus, which causes some theological problems).

A revision, the New Revised Standard Version (1990), was produced with the co-operation of Roman Catholic, Protestant, Orthodox and Jewish scholars. This made use of new discoveries of papyri, advances in textual reconstruction and especially the Hebrew texts of Isaiah and Habakkuk, newly discovered at Qumran, and the extensive fragments of the Hebrew text of Ben Sira found at Qumran and on Massada. It caused controversy, and failed to win acceptance in some circles, by its uncompromising use of inclusive language, to the extent of changing singulars into plurals ('their' avoids 'his/her') and the addition to 'brothers' of 'and sisters' when the translators considered that a text was addressed to women as well as men. The story-telling of the Old Testament is often scintillating, and a number of the solutions to translation problems can only be described as brilliant. Some very sensitive decisions were taken, such as to retain the distinction between 'shall' and 'will' in the more classic language of the Old Testament, but to abandon it in the more colloquial language of the New.

Nevertheless, there remains a certain staidness about the translation which betrays that it is still a revision of a revision of the King James Version. In all Bible translations two compromises must be faced. The first is between readability and verbal accuracy: a readable translation often has to depart from the exact words and the shape of the original sentence. The second is that a phrase in the original may be so obscure as to be tolerant of more than one meaning, so that the translator has to rule out the ambiguity and opt for a single clear meaning. On both these matters I find that a good balance is achieved by the NRSV.

The Jerusalem Bible and New Jerusalem Bible

The RSV was closely followed by the Roman Catholic Jerusalem Bible, in 1966 the first translation of the whole Bible into fully modern English, the work of a distinguished literary panel under the editorship of Alexander Jones. For instance the 66 chapters of the Book of Isaiah were translated in two weeks by the actor Robert Speaight, who knew neither Greek nor Hebrew – or so he told me. J.R.R. Tolkien points out that to name him among the principal collaborators of the Jerusalem Bible 'was an undeserved courtesy', since he only translated the Book of Jonah and 'was consulted on one or two points of style'.[2] The parent Bible de Jérusalem was begun in 1946 at the French Catholic Biblical School in Jerusalem, and was intended to incorporate the important advances in Roman Catholic biblical scholarship this century. The books, copiously annotated and introduced, were published first in separate fascicles over ten years. The English Jerusalem Bible, having no basis in traditional English versions, has the freshness of freedom from traditional biblical language. For Catholics it rapidly supplanted the antiquated Rheims-Douai version. Perhaps the most controversial feature was the use of 'Yahweh' for the divine name, which was excoriated as a reversion to a mere local, tribal deity. It was basically a translation from the Bible de Jérusalem, conceived primarily to convey to the English-speaking world the biblical scholarship of this French Bible. The translation of the text was originally no more than a vehicle for the notes.

The New Jerusalem Bible, published 1985, was edited by the present writer. The notes and introductions were brought more or less[3] up to that date, and the accuracy of the translation considerably improved. Despite claims to the contrary, it is clear that the Jerusalem Bible was translated from the French, possibly with occasional glances at the Hebrew or Greek, rather than vice versa. For the NJB the opposite was the case, with some books being translated completely afresh. It was the first complete Bible to make consistent use of inclusive language wherever possible, though without the extreme rigour of the later NRSV.

In France, however, the Bible de Jérusalem had its own special importance. After centuries of division between Protestants and Catholics over translations of the Bible, following the Second Vatican Council (1962–1965), agreement was reached in 1968 between the Vatican and the United Bible Societies over a set of principles for translation. Following these principles the Bible de Jérusalem formed the basis for the first French ecumenical version of the Bible, the Traduction Oecuménique de la Bible. In

Germany also the Einheitsübersetzung was launched jointly by Catholic cardinal and Protestant bishop in 1980. In the French and German-speaking countries respectively these two translations now hold the field with little competition. No such agreement has yet been reached in English-speaking lands.

The New English Bible and Revised English Bible

The New English Bible, initiated by the Church of Scotland in 1946 and completed in 1970, was an attempt to break away from the mould of 'biblical English' associated with the tradition stemming from Tyndale. It also deliberately eschewed any effort consistently to translate the same word in the original Greek or Hebrew by the same English word. There is an impressive freshness and modernity about this version which reflects the eagerness of the translators to bring home the meaning of the text to a reader unused to the traditional language of the Bible. An interesting feature was the adoption of many unusual readings of the Hebrew: there are many occasions where the Hebrew text uses a word which occurs only once or twice, and whose meaning is therefore pretty obscure. On hundreds of occasions the NEB used fresh and untried scholarly suggestions (utilizing similar words known from other related languages) to give a meaning to these. This was heavily criticised as 'eccentric and idiosyncratic',[4] and many of these were removed in the revision, e.g. at Judges 1:14:

NEB: As she sat on the ass she broke wind, and Caleb said, 'What did you mean by that?'

REB: She dismounted from her donkey, and Caleb asked her, What do you want?'

It was revised as the Revised English Bible in 1989, with participation (at least notional) from the Bible Society and most of the mainstream churches of the British Isles. This united ecclesiastical participation has not, however, enabled it to overcome all competition; indeed the REB is not one of the versions authorised for use in Roman Catholic churches. Nevertheless, some of the solutions to translation problems are breathtakingly apt, though the avoidance of all semitic 'biblical' language has sometimes led to accusations of paraphrase rather than translation.

The Good News Bible/Today's English Version

Among the most widely-used versions is The Good News Bible (completed 1976), sponsored by the American Bible Society, prepared by the United Bible Society and published on both sides of the Atlantic in slightly different versions. The American title, Today's English Version, and especially the British sub-title, Today's Good News, reflect its purpose accurately, for dignity and literary quality have been sacrificed to the desire to make the Bible accessible to those whose English is less sophisticated. Since it is 'intended for all who use English as a means of communication the translators have tried to avoid words and forms not in current or widespread use' (Preface). This 'effort to use language that is natural, clear, simple and unambiguous' and 'at the elementary school reading level' has led to a certain impoverishment of the rich traditional biblical vocabulary and a consequent loss of depth in theology and communication. It is a determined effort to move out of the biblical world and culture ('the Covenant Box' replaces 'the Ark of the Covenant'), even to the extent of tabulating or condensing into a few phrases verses which are judged unimportant (Numbers 7:12–88). The price paid is a certain loss of richness and imagery, when God's 'right hand' and his 'mighty arm' become simply his 'power'. Oddly enough, the almost meaningless 'righteousness' is retained (e.g. Romans 3:26), while the theological impoverishment comes out in avoidance of such terms as 'reconciliation', e.g. at 2 Corinthians 5:19.

NJB: God was in Christ ... entrusting to us the message of reconciliation.

REB: God ... has entrusted us with the message of reconciliation.

GNB/TEV: Our message is that God was making all mankind his friends.

This version certainly has its uses as a first introduction to the Bible for young people and for those for whom English is a second language. It is the only major Bible illustrated throughout, richly and aptly, with thoughtful and witty line-drawings, which combine humour with reverence.

The New American Standard Bible

An interesting Bible with a special purpose is the New American
Standard Bible. This is a revision of the 1901 American Standard
Bible, sponsored by the Lockman Foundation in California and
produced in 1971 'with the conviction that the words of Scripture
as originally penned in the Greek and Hebrew were inspired by
God' (Preface). The claim to objectivity of translation is so strong
that the names of the scholars responsible for it were not released
until 2002. The care to reflect the original words is visible every-
where. If the translators judged that they had inserted a word
which was not in the original, this word was put in italics; this
frequently occurs with the verb 'to be' which can often be
omitted in both Hebrew and Greek where English requires it. If a
historic present in Greek is rendered by a past tense in English,
this is signalled by an asterisk, e.g. 'says' may become '*said'. The
reverence for the text is impressive: in a dozen places the NASB
uses the Dead Sea Scroll text of Isaiah, but only when it is
confirmed by the Greek version or another parallel passage.[5]
Similarly, it claims not to interpret, so retains the original even at
the price of obscurity: at 1 Thessalonians 4:4 the Greek word
translated rather meaninglessly by NASB as 'vessel' normally
means 'thing', 'kit', 'apparatus', here and frequently in an
obviously euphemistic sense:

NRSV: each one of you knows how to control his own body in
holiness and honour.

NJB: each one of you to know how to control his body in a way
that is holy and honourable.

REB: each one of you must learn to gain mastery over his body
to hallow and honour it.

NASB: each of you know how to possess his own vessel in
sanctification and honour.

On the other hand objectivity flies right out of the window
when it comes to Christology. One of the four principles of translation is 'They shall give the Lord Jesus Christ His proper place,
the place which the Word gives Him'. At Isaiah 7:14 the Hebrew
has a word meaning 'young girl'. Matthew 1:23 follows the Greek
translation (one of the passages which has led many to hold that
the LXX translation is 'inspired', for this is clearly an interpretation) in using 'virgin'. NASB goes one better, and puts 'virgin' in

Isaiah. In the same vein it inserts the definite article at the centurion's confession, 'Truly this was *the* Son of God' (Mark 15:39). The Greek has no article, and the delicacy of the Markan irony is that the pagan centurion makes a pagan statement on one plane which the Christian reader understands on another plane. Similarly, the capitalization of 'Son' is one of a host of instances where the NASB capitalizes to inform the reader that the deity is intended, e.g. 'From you One will go forth for Me to be ruler in Israel' (Micah 5:2). This translation is a noble effort, true to its principles, but must be approached with a certain reserve.

The New American Bible

Finally a word must be said about the New American Bible, which could perhaps be described as the official American Roman Catholic version. The current version is an amalgam, the Old Testament completed in 1970, with a psalter revised in 1991. The 1970 version was heavily criticised,[6] which led to a revision of the New Testament so radical that it approximates to a new translation. This New Testament was published in 1986. However, two features of the translation were disallowed by Vatican guidelines in 1997 and 2001, the use of dynamic equivalence[7] and of inclusive language. For the liturgy, therefore, a new translation, the Amended Revised New American Bible, was created, which includes only those passages used in the liturgy. A distinguished panel of American Catholic scholars has been appointed, who are currently engaged on the work of revision.

SEVEN

The Bible and Vatican II

Sola Scriptura *or Two Sources of Revelation?*

The chapters in this book have discussed the Bible as a text, how the different books came to be considered 'Bible' and the hesitations about various components, some of which ended outside the collection, others inside the collection; how that text came from Greek and Hebrew into Latin, and then into English (with a glance at other modern languages); how the most widely diffused of all English texts, probably the most widely diffused of all Bibles, the King James Version, came into existence. The purpose of this final chapter is to see how the Bible, which has come down to us by such a varied path, actually communicates with us. Christians have been called 'the people of the Book'; why is the Book so precious? We have left it till the end to discuss what the whole process is about.

A book does not exist on its own. Its author is wanting to say something, to communicate something. At the very least there is a sponsoring body, which owns the book. The saying quoted above may be reversed: as well as Christians being the people of the book, the book is the book of the people, Christians. Just as the book defines the people, so the people define the book. At the very beginning there was a sense that the oral tradition in the Church was more authoritative than the written tradition. In the centuries when decisions were being made about which books belonged to the Bible and which did not, there was an interplay between text and living tradition. The Bible was the book of the Church, and the Church authorities decided what was part of the Bible and what was not. We have records in some instances of bishops or Church councils making the decisions. More frequently the decisions just happened. That is, some books were considered fit for reading in church and others not. Formal decisions by Church councils confirmed, or merely expressed, common practice.

A decisive break occurred at the Reformation, when Luther rejected Church tradition and embraced the principle of *sola scriptura*. Luther insisted that scripture was sufficient of itself: 'I want scripture alone to rule, and not to be interpreted according to my spirit or that of any other man, but to be understood in its own light'.[1] Again and again he maintains that scripture is clear and needs no interpretation: 'The word of God does not need to be forced in any way either by men or by angels. Rather, its plainest meanings are to be preserved, and the words are not to be understood apart from their proper and literal sense'.[2] Luther is fulminating against some abuses in ecclesiastical practice (the denial to the laity of communion under both kinds) and some theological developments (the Aristotelian/Thomist analysis of the presence of Christ in the eucharist in terms of 'transsubstantiation'). The obvious difficulty in Luther's principle as stated is that different readers understand the same written words in different senses. Luther's principle fails because scripture read 'in its own light' means different things to different people. There is no denying that there were abuses in Church practice and that the understanding of scripture was widely distorted at the end of the medieval period by all kinds of allegorical arabesques. But every thoughtful reader of a life-giving text will reflect on it and draw out its implications, not always in the same sense.

It is naïve to claim that scripture always has a 'plainest meaning'. The discussions and disagreements in the earliest centuries of the Church about the implications of 'the word was made flesh' leave no doubt about this. Does the Word made flesh have one nature or two? Is he wholly human? Did God die on the cross? Has he a human mind and will, and how are his human mind and will related to the divine mind and will? Has he a human personality? Decisions on such matters which go far beyond the 'plainest meanings' of scripture are enshrined in the decision of early councils, and were eventually accepted by the whole, or nearly the whole, of Christendom. There are still important bodies of Christians who are classed by the numerical majority of Christians as Nestorians or Monophysites. More serious, because more practical, different bodies of Christians understand in a different sense the 'plainest meaning' of the words at the Last Supper, 'This is my body ... this is my blood.' Some hold that the eucharistic bread and wine become in some sense the body and blood of Christ; others that Christ is bodily received by the reception of the bread and wine, still others that the bread and wine are mere symbolic reminders of Jesus' last meal with his disciples on the eve of his Passion. Each of these understandings of scripture is held by its adherents to constitute the 'plainest meaning' of the words. The disagreements and fragmentation produced from the earliest years by the Lutheran appeal to the 'plainest meaning' of scripture become evident in the variety of understandings of the eucharist among the Reformers,[3] in the differences about whether the prohibition of graven images in the Ten Commandments forbids all statuary and religious art, in the controversy whether it is possible to administer baptism to infants despite the fact that in the New Testament it is exclusively an adult expression of faith.[4]

The Roman Catholic reply to Luther's preference for the 'plainest meaning' of scripture was given, in characteristically stern language, at what was in fact the first full working session of the Council of Trent in April 1546:

> The council further decrees, in order to control those of unbalanced character, that no one shall dare to interpret the sacred scriptures either by twisting its text to his individual meaning in opposition to that which has been and is held by holy mother church, whose function it is to pass judgment on the true meaning and interpretation of the sacred scriptures, or by giving it meanings contrary to the unanimous consent of the fathers.[5]

The council's statement can certainly be read to imply two separate sources of doctrine: 'this truth and this discipline are contained in written books and in unwritten traditions which were received by the apostles from the lips of Christ himself' (Tanner 1990, p. 664). Indeed over the course of time it became common teaching that there were two independent sources of revelation, one being scripture, the other being tradition, as though some sacred truths were contained in one of these sources, others in the other. So in 1950 Pius XII could write in his encyclical *Humani generis*:

> Theologians must always return to the founts of revelation. It is their task to show how the teachings of the living magisterium are contained in Holy Writ and in sacred tradition either explicitly or implicitly. In addition, that each of the two sources of divinely revealed doctrine contains so

many and such great treasures of truth that it can never be exhausted.[6]

In practice, however, it must be stressed that these two sources were not treated separately. For instance, in the definition of the Assumption of Mary, made by Pius XII four months later, the preamble runs: 'All these arguments and considerations of the Fathers and of theologians rest on Holy Scripture as their basic foundation...' before going on to discuss arguments from tradition from as early as the second century. Nevertheless, there remained an uneasy feeling in relationships between Roman Catholics and Protestants that Catholics had up their sleeves a whole collection of doctrines which were not contained in scripture, and could be substantiated only from more or less well-founded traditions. So the situation remained until the decisive event of the Second Vatican Council.

Vatican II: the Background to the Council
In 1959 the aged but recently-elected Pope John XXII decided that he would hold a Council of the Church for the purpose of *aggiornamento*, bringing the Church up to date, into the world of the present day (*giorno* is the Italian for 'day'). Born of a peasant family in the foothills of the Italian Alps, Angelo Roncalli had wide experience of the Church in Europe and of its quarrels. As a young priest he had travelled widely as secretary to the bishop of Bergamo. Later he had had experience of Eastern Christianity as representative of the pope in Bulgaria, Turkey and Greece during the Second World War. At the end of that war he was made papal nuncio or ambassador to France, replacing the ambassador whose co-operation with the pro-German Vichy Government made him no longer acceptable in post-war France. In Paris particularly Giuseppe Roncalli established a reputation for conciliation and warmth (as well as good cooking). After a brief period as archbishop of Venice he had been elected to the papacy in old age, as a harmless stopgap, never expecting to make the dramatic moves which were to come.

One of John XXII's principal emphases, if not the principal emphasis, once he had declared that he would hold a council of the Church, and as the council approached, was Church unity.

From the beginning he changed the established Vatican language, eschewing the language of 're-union', which automatically stressed the need for non-Catholics to 'return to the fold', and preferring to speak of separated brethren who should join in seeking the unity which Christ is preparing for us. Within months he formed the important Secretariat for Promoting Christian Unity, which was to check all the council documents. Building on his wartime experience of the Eastern Church, he sent an ambassador to Istanbul, Athens and Alexandria to invite representatives to attend the council, and in turn sent observers to the 1961 meeting of the World Council of Churches. Working with other Christians was clearly going to be an important part of letting in the new day, and this would have a decisive effect on the development of the council, the topics discussed and the way they were treated, including the discussion of scripture and revelation. At the heart of many of the disagreements between Christians was the issue of authority and the access to Christian truth.

Preparation for the council limped unevenly. On the one hand the commission charged with the preparation sent round to 2,593 bishops – and all the bishops of the Universal (i.e. Catholic) Church were summoned to the council – questionnaires and discussion papers. On the other hand the papal bureaucracy or *Curia* (a word which suggests the royal court of an absolute monarch) saw the council not as an instrument for radical change but as an anodyne synod for tidying up a few loose ends. Headed by the seventy-two-year-old Cardinal Ottaviani, the Congregation for Doctrine prepared five major *schemata*, or discussion documents, for presentation and approval by the bishops assembling for the council. It also 'helpfully' proposed a list of names of those who were to serve on the ten co-ordinating commissions, who would consider the amendments proposed in discussion in the council chamber. Each commission was to have 24 members, 16 elected by the members of the council and 8 nominated by the pope. If the council Fathers had behaved themselves and elected their representatives from these proposed lists, things would have gone smoothly for the *curia*.

On the opening day of discussion at the council, however, 13 October 1962, a radical revolt exploded. The council Fathers, led by a powerful group of European cardinals, including cardinals Liénart of Lille, Frings of Cologne and Alfrink of Utrecht, refused to vote on the names proposed, explaining that they had just come together from all over the world and needed time to get to know one another and to discern the suitable experts in each field. This was the first evidence of a split which was to dominate at least the early sessions of the council, between the conservative papal *curia* and more progressive elements. The bishop of Cuernavaca compared St Peter's to a giant pressure-cooker which transformed the outlook of the bishops of the entire world; he might have added, 'and often seemed in danger of exploding'.

One incident from the margins may serve as illustration: in the run-up to the council two professors at the Pontifical Biblical Insitute were dismissed on papal authority for 'unorthodoxy'.[7] The principal of the Institute resigned in sympathy. One of the two professors, Stanislaus Lyonnet, remarked to me the following year that his dismissal had been providential, for otherwise he would not have had time to lecture on biblical topics to the French bishops assembled in Rome. Two years later the new principal asked the pope (who seemed unaware of their dismissal) that they should be reinstated. The pope instructed him to proceed through Ottaviani, who felt obliged to concede. But as the principal left the room Ottaviani said to him (in Latin) 'What you have to do, do quickly' – the words of Jesus to Judas, as Judas left the room of the Last Supper to perpetrate his act of betrayal, a nicely barbed allusion.[8] This incident illustrates well the quiet internal struggles which were going on behind the scenes. One German adviser[9] remarked to me, 'The Holy Spirit is at work in the Council Chamber. Outside it, we manage things'.

The First Schema on the Bible

In November began consideration of the schema, or discussion document, on the Bible. It was called *De Fontibus Revelationis*, by the use of the plural in the title itself accepting the two sources of revelation, namely scripture and tradition, as two separate sources of knowledge of God.

Discussion in the council chamber was, of course, still in Latin, with rare exceptions. Right from the beginning Maximos IV, Patriarch of Tyre, insisted on speaking French, pointing out that Latin was not the language of the Church, only the language of the *Western* Church.[10] The schema was presented by Cardinal

Ottaviani, as president of the Roman Congregation for Doctrine. (He had been absent from the council for two weeks, upset at having his microphone switched off when he had spoken for nearly double the maximum time allotted for speeches.) He was supported by two other Italian cardinals who were well known for their conservatism, Ruffini of Palermo and Siri of Genoa. When discussion started, the document was savaged. The Melkite (Greek) archbishop Neofito Edelby pointed out that the whole approach was dominated by the polemic of the Reformation in its opposition to Luther's principle of *sola scriptura*. Bishop de Smedt of the Church Unity Commission denounced it for triumphalism, clericalism and legalism; it was backward–looking and defensive. Bishop Charrue of Namur compared it to the Church's stance on Galileo for its refusal to accept the findings of modern science. Bishop Hakim of Akko (Acre in Palestine) attested that the division into two sources of tradition had never been accepted in the eastern Church. When these criticisms were reinforced by the big guns of Cardinals Liénart, Frings, Alfrink, Ritter (of St Louis, Missouri) and Bea (head of the Church Unity Commission, formerly head of the Roman Biblical Institute, so a noted biblical scholar), the schema was withdrawn, to be revised by a special commission jointly headed by Ottaviani and Bea. The head of the English Benedictines, Abbot Christopher Butler, also worked as a member of the panel.

The Revised Schema, Dei Verbum

A New Focus

When the new and revised schema came to be debated in September of the following year, 1964, it was found to have an altogether different focus. The focus was no longer on the biblical revelation of a package of intellectual truths, as though revelation was primarily a set of propositions about God. Revelation was no longer a matter of the unveiling of truths; it was a matter of the acceptance of a gift. Revelation is seen as a divine act of self-revelation, God's own self-disclosure, made not only to the mind but also to the heart. It is therefore God's self-giving, for in biblical language to 'know' is used of a warm and personal relationship, often including sexual knowledge (when Adam 'knew'

Eve, Genesis 4:1, 17, 25, etc). 'I love you' is more than a statement of fact; it is a declaration. It involves a personal commitment. So the revelation in scripture is the offering or communication of a person, the self-giving of a person, demanding a response in faith. God 'in his great love speaks to humankind as friends and enters into their life, so as to invite and receive them into relationship with himself'.

The first quotation from scripture, in the opening sentence, is about having fellowship with God (1 John 1:2–3), and the whole emphasis of the first chapter is on God speaking to humankind as friends, inviting them into a relationship with God. Revelation is a matter of life and hope, not of understanding truths, for from the beginning God 'roused our first parents to hope for salvation by the promise of redemption'. The fullness of revelation is in Jesus, not only in his teaching but in the total reality of his presence, his symbolic acts and above all his death and resurrection. Again, it is getting to know a person rather than a set of facts. The human response is not assent to doctrines but acknowledging God and 'free self-commitment to God'. The reception of revelation is not an intellectual experience so much as a life-experience, an entering into a partnership or an 'uninterrupted conversation' with God.

Only after this general framework has been established is it possible to go on to discuss particular questions to which this framework provides a starting-point. How were specific books chosen, why were these four gospels chosen rather than the single expurgated gospel of Luke favoured by Marcion or the additional sayings of the Gospel of Thomas? Four criteria seem to have been in use in the earliest times, no single one of which was absolute:[11]

- Apostolic, stemming from the earliest times. It was important that the author should be a *vir apostolicus*, though neither Mark nor Luke even claims to have been one of the Twelve. The Vatican II document considers this category of 'apostolic men' to be wider than the Twelve (no. 7), and perhaps deliberately does not define it more closely.
- Catholic (in the sense of 'universal'), applicable to the Church as a whole, not necessarily written for the Christian community as a whole (which would exclude Paul's letters), but of

universal relevance, rather than of particular relevance for a particular group, such as monks or deaconnesses.

● Orthodox, that is, in accordance with the tradition, which sees 'the two testaments like a mirror in which the Church during its pilgrimage on earth contemplates God, the source of all that it has received' (no. 7).

● Traditional, that is, used from the earliest times.

The scripture is part of the total experience of God in Christ, and those books remained central and guaranteed by the Church which were felt to express what Christians saw as the expression of that relationship. To use the influential expression of Karl Rahner, 'the writings of the New Testament originate as life-processes of the Church; they are sediments of that which in her has been transmitted and preached as her faith'.[12]

Foundation Documents of the Church

In the process of the 'sediment' settling down, other documents fell away. Among these are those Infancy Gospels which show the young Jesus making clay pigeons, clapping his hands and watching them fly away,[13] or withering up another child who spoils his game. One may deduce that these were just stories, and this was not the Christ who was judged to be the expression of the divine self-giving in revelation. This Jesus was not the Jesus whom the Christian Church knew, not part of the mirror in which the Church contemplates God; they are not elements in the life-processes of the Church. The first instance of a reason given for excluding a gospel from the books to be read in church precisely corresponds to this: a Gospel of Peter was being read at Rhossus, but was excluded by Bishop Serapion in the late second century on the grounds that it was docetic,[14] that is, it did not correspond to the Church's view of Christ.

How did the Church know this, and what right had any particular group to judge this? One can only say that the experience of Christ was passed on, for God 'still maintains an uninterrupted conversation with the bride of his beloved Son' (no. 8). Profoundly felt is the continuing tradition within the Church: 'This tradition which comes from the apostles progresses in the Church under the assistance of the holy Spirit. There is a growth in understanding of what is handed on, both the words and the realities they signify' (no. 8). The Bible remains the book of the Church, and there is a living co-relationship or conversation between tradition entrusted to the apostles by Christ and their successors, so that 'both scripture and tradition are to be accepted and honoured with like devotion and reverence' (no. 9).

A clear position had been taken on this matter by the original schema in its plural title, *On the Sources of Revelation*. In the very beginning of discussion this position was stigmatised as 'dominated by Reformation polemic', since it openly implies that there are two independent sources of revelation, scripture and tradition.[15] So in the same vein, during the discussion of the revised schema in the following year, the conservative Cardinal Florit asked for the statement to be inserted, 'Not every Catholic doctrine can be proved from scripture alone'. This would have left open the possible implication that proof from tradition without scriptural evidence suffices. It was not inserted, but a subtly different statement replaced it: 'the Church does not derive through scripture alone her certitude about all that has been revealed' (no. 9). The subject is now not proof but understanding. The full range of understanding is not derived merely from unaided poring over, delving into the scriptures, but 'is a process to which tradition contributes'.[16] In a prolonged discussion of the matter, the council Fathers refused to make any statement about the proportionate contribution of scripture and tradition, holding that theological discussion had not progressed sufficiently far.

In the end the document (no. 10) indicates this refusal to make any exclusive decision,[17] laying the stress inclusively on three factors: the teaching authority, a devoted attention to the scriptures and a single deposit of faith:

> The task of authentically interpreting the word of God, whether in its written form or in that of tradition, has been entrusted only to those charged with the church's ongoing teaching function, whose authority is exercised in the name of Jesus Christ. This teaching function is not above the word of God but stands at its service, teaching nothing but what is handed down, according as it devotedly listens, reverently preserves and faithfully transmits the word of God. All that it proposes for belief, as being divinely revealed, is drawn from the one deposit of faith.

Inerrancy

The same eirenic approach[18] was used for another topic of controversy, the inerrancy of the Bible. Can the Bible contain errors? Since the discoveries of science began to impinge on the reading of the Bible, the problem of inerrancy has spiralled. Galileo pointed out astronomical difficulties: how can the sun stand still (Joshua 10:12)? Darwin pointed up terrestrial ones: how does the account of creation square with the facts of evolution? A great deal of ink was spilt and a great deal of heat generated in the attempt to formulate the way in which the Bible was without error. Was it without error only in matters of faith and morality? What were the limits of these, anyway? The early chapters of Genesis certainly do not teach about history, physics or biology. The gospels make mistakes about history (the census in Luke 2:2). Jesus himself is historically wrong in ascribing the authorship of the psalms to David (Mark 12:37). This question too was left blandly open: 'we must acknowledge that the books of scripture teach firmly, faithfully and without error such truth as God, for the sake of our salvation, wished the biblical text to contain' (no. 11). Wisely, it does not list which these truths are! Nor, indeed, would this be consistent with the more general position that revelation is the self-gift of a person, drawing human beings into a personal relationship with God. Such a self-gift does not occur merely through communication of truths. To quote again Bishop Butler:

> Is it not reasonable to make the notion of divine authorship as wide in its scope as that of human authorship? We know, in fact, that human authors are not always making assertions claimed to be 'true'. They do not only affirm; they exhort, they exult or lament, they express in other words, not only truths but emotions, they 'edify' not only their reader's intellect but his sensibility and his spirit'.[19]

Yet again, this is a way in which Vatican II, instead of searching out points of doctrine on which there is disagreement among Christians, and condemning those who disagreed, sought to assert what is agreed among Christians, and to leave open to further investigation and discussion questions on which theologians of many traditions agree.

Use of the Bible

The final chapter of *Dei Verbum* can be seen as the most important of its six chapters[20] since it outlines how the teaching and attitudes of the previous chapters should form life in the Church, that is, How the Bible Comes to Us.

For Roman Catholics this was a novelty, for the Bible had been neglected in the recent life of the Church. It had become widely regarded as the preserve of Protestants, not exactly forbidden territory, but dangerous and probably barren as well. At the Reformation all the stress of the Reformers had been on the Bible as the single source of authority and teaching, *sola scriptura*, coupled with and resulting in a flight from other factors of Church life, such as tradition and liturgy, sometimes also – as in the Puritan movements and in much of Calvinism – from beauty of art, drama and architecture.

This is no place to enter into apologetics for either side. Suffice to say that there were, in the sixteenth century, as in every other century, plenty of abuses:

- allegorical interpretations which detracted from the direct message of the scripture. Luther's example is Origen's treating the trees of the Garden of Eden as allegories, 'since hence it might be inferred that trees were not created by God' (*On the Babylonish Captivity of the Church*, p. 312).
- traditional practices and ceremonies which had acquired an independent importance out of all proportion to their value. An excellent example of this is the preference for canon law above scripture, leading to the attitude which so riled William Tyndale (p. 75).
- liturgical arabesques which had lost their meaning and obscured the essentials of the liturgy. Local rites of eucharistic practice had developed, in which the essentials were obscured by a blanket of ceremony (in England, the Sarum Rite). Reception of the sacrament had become rare, and the chalice was – one of Luther's strong objections[21] – denied to the laity.
- a tradition of wall-painting and other illustration – one of the

most important means of instruction for the illiterate – which concentrated on the lurid, especially the Last Judgement and the fires of Hell, to the extent of distorting the orientation of the message.

● elaborate dramatic processions (particularly at Shrovetide and Holy Week), more popular and drawing much more attention than more sober liturgies; Mystery Plays inspired more by legend and apocryphal stories than by the canonical scripture.

Many of these florid traditional developments were pruned away both by the Protestant Reformers on the one side and the Catholic Counter-Reformation on the other. Nevertheless, one of the results of the Reformation was a parting of the ways in which Catholics took refuge in the sacraments to the neglect of the scripture no less than Protestants took refuge in scripture to the neglect of sacramental life, both sides rather priding themselves on the neglect of the other element.

A second factor which had led to neglect of the Bible in the Roman Catholic Church was a suspicion resulting from the Catholic Modernist Movement in the first decade of the twentieth century. As a result of the interpretation put upon the archaeological and literary studies of the nineteenth century by some Catholic scholars,[22] notably Alfred Loisy, a vigorous movement to check excesses in Catholic biblical studies was spearheaded by the Pontifical Biblical Commission in a series of repressive measures from 1905 till 1918. Every diocese was instructed to set up an anti-Modernist Commission. Every priest ordained, every student receiving a theological degree, every Catholic teacher of theology had repeatedly to swear the anti-Modernist oath.[23] It was only in 1943, with the papal encyclical *Divino Afflante Spiritu*, that cautious progress could again be resumed, only in 1948 that a letter to Cardinal Suhard of Paris allowed the opinion that Adam and Eve were not real, historical persons, and only in 1955 that the repressive decrees of the Pontifical Biblical Commission were withdrawn. There was an atmosphere of caution and fear which did not encourage too much use of the Bible. Clergy and theologians trained in the first quarter, or even half, of the twentieth century regarded biblical studies, and particularly study of the Old Testament, as a minefield into which it was better not to stray. Typical was the comment made to a student by an English bishop in the first year of the Vatican II, 'You are studying the Bible? I suppose that means you don't believe in it?'[24]

This was a far cry from the statement of *Dei Verbum*, no. 21:

> There is such force and power in the word of God that it stands as the church's support and strength, affording her children sturdiness in faith, food for the soul and a pure and unfailing fount of spiritual life.

Or from the statement of no. 23 that theologians should take all appropriate means to study the bible:

> So that ministers of the word may be able, as widely as possible, to nourish God's people with the food of the scriptures, and so produce the effect of enlightening minds, strengthening wills and firing hearts with the love of God.

The decree *Dei Verbum* put an end to the negative attitudes to the scriptures. It was no longer possible to maintain the strife between scripture and tradition, and the scripture was seen to be one part of the ongoing life of the Church, an integral element in every activity and every direction. Just two direct consequences of this renewal may be outlined:

- *Dei Verbum* 22 directly encouraged ecumenical collaboration over the Bible: 'If the opportunity arises, and church authority approves, such versions [translations] may be prepared in collaboration with Christians of other denominations; all Christians will then be able to use them.' Such co-operation on editions of the Bible has issued in significant translations, such as the NRSV. More significant still, it has removed wider suspicions between churches, leading to wider co-operation and mutual understanding.
- *Dei Verbum* 25 insists: 'Let it never be forgotten that prayer should accompany the reading of holy scripture, so that it becomes a dialogue between God and the human reader; for "when we pray, we talk to him: when we read the divine word, we listen to him" [Ambrose, *De Officiis Ministrorum*, I.20.88].' This has led to a revaluation of the reading of scripture as part of prayer, for example, at the beginning of any Christian meet-

ing. It has made possible a biblically-based service of public prayer where the celebration of the Eucharist is impossible or inappropriate, enabling a meeting and dialogue with God where previously none would have been possible.

In conclusion the conclusion of the document may be quoted: 'Just as faithful and frequent reception of the eucharistic mystery makes the church's life grow, so we may hope that its spiritual life will receive a new impulse from increased devotion to the word of God, which "abides for ever"'.

NOTES

Chapter 1: How Did the Bible Come into Being?

1. Cavallin 1974, pp. 103–104, cf. Wright 2003, p. 148.
2. Moule 1962, p. 8.
3. E.g. Casey 1998.
4. J. Kloppenborg Verbin 2000.
5. Massively by Robinson 1976 and 1985.
6. Lagrange 1985, p. 55.
7. Read-Heimerdinger, 2002, p. 348.
8. Elliott and Moir 1995, p. 4.

Chapter 2: A Process of Selection

1. A good example of the products of the Jesus Seminar is Gerd Lüdemann's *Jesus after 2000 Years*. A thorough criticism of its methods is given by Luke Timothy Johnson in Johnson 1996, pp. 1–27, and by Witherington 1995, pp. 42–57. Briefly, it is a seminar of like-minded North American fellows, not including any from Yale, Harvard, Princeton, Duke or any Catholic university. In no way does it represent a cross-section of scholars. It met regularly during the 1980s and 1990s, with maximum possible publicity, to vote with coloured beads on the likelihood of individual Jesus-sayings actually being from Jesus. Only 18% got through.
2. See the article by Ron Cameron in *Anchor Bible Dictionary*, 'Thomas, Gospel of'.
3. Hurtado 2003, pp. 452–474.
4. Pagels 1979, p. xviii.
5. The strangest fragment of all deserves a footnote. Professor Morton Smith 1973, p. 17, claims to have discovered in 1958 in the monastery of Mar Saba in the Judaean desert a fragment of a letter of Clement of Alexandria, quoting The Secret Gospel of Mark as follows: 'After six days Jesus told him [a youth] what to do, and in the evening the youth comes to him, wearing a linen cloth over his naked body. And he remained with him that night, for Jesus taught him the mystery of the kingdom of God. And thence, arising, he returned to the other side of the Jordan'. Scandal-mongers have, of course, made much of this text, but to this day it has proved impossible to authenticate it.
6. See *Anchor Bible Dictionary* vol. 4, 'Marcion, Bible of'.
7. See Kinzig 1994, 519–544.
8. *New Jerome Commentary*, p. 1044, #55.
9. *Inspiration in the Bible* (Herder, 1961).

10. Minns 1994, p. 132.
11. Vallée 1980, p. 185.
12. For the text (PG 26, 1436) see Brakke, 1995, p. 329.

Chapter 3: St Jerome and the Vulgate

1. See the list in the NRSV cross-reference edition (OUP 2003), pp. vi–vii.
2. Sparks 1970, pp. 510–547.
3. I was similarly taunted in Jerusalem in September 2004 by two Orthodox Jews, who mocked the Christians for thinking that there were 72 elders, not 70 (Exodus 24:1). They were unconvinced by my appeal to textual variants in Luke 10:1.
4. It is most conveniently available in the splendid edition edited (with a charmingly mannered Latin introduction) by Frederick Field, *Origenis Hexaplorum quae supersunt* (OUP, 1875). The original was probably destroyed in the sack of Caesarea by the Persians in the early seventh century.
5. The comment and examples of this excessive literalism are given by Field, pp. xxi–xxiii. Rahlfs is more outspoken: 'He did not shrink from perpetrating the most appalling outrages to the whole essence of the Greek language' (Preface to the Stuttgart edition of the LXX, p. xxiv).
6. *Ep ad Afric.* 4
7. In modern editions of the Vulgate (e.g. the Salamanca edition [*Biblioteca de autores cristianos*, 1965]) the Gallican Psalter and the revision of 1945 are printed side by side.
8. The fuss seems to have been about the plant which God produced to shade Jonah in Jonah 4:6. In his *Commentary on Jonah* Jerome suggests that the standard translation was 'ivy'. He points out that this provides meagre shade, and prefers a gourd-type plant, *cucurbita*, which grows quickly in Palestine. Modern translations have settled for a castor-oil plant. The Greek has κολοκυνθηφ.
9. Jerome was 9 years older than Augustine. In 404 Jerome was 59 years old; he was to live another 16 years.
10. Mynors, 1937, I.12.3, p. 37.
11. Some 40 kg , according to Bruce-Mitford 1967, p. 2.

Chapter 4: The Bible in English

1. *Surtees Society*, London, vols xvi and xix (1845 and 1847).
2. Ed. Colgrave 1958.
3. Crawford 1922.
4. Deanesly 1920, p. 193
5. Raine 1839, p. 118.
6. Wright 1845, vol 1.43.
7. Deanesley 1920, p. 62.
8. Kenelm Foster, ibid., p. 455.

9. Lumby 1895, vol. 2, p. 151.
10. *De Ecclesia*, ed. J. Loserth, 366.
11. *De Veritate Sacrae Scripturae*, ed. R. Buddensieg, 117, 382–384.
12. Quoted in *Anchor Bible Dictionary* 6, p. 818.
13. E.g. A. Kenny, *Wyclif, the morning star of the Reformation* (OUP, 1985).
14. Letter to Erasmus, *Complete Works of Erasmus*, tr. R. A. B. Mynors (Toronto, University of Toronto Press), 26.
15. The estimate of David Daniell (*William Tyndale* [Yale UP, 1994], p. 396).
16. One such book is the *Biblia Pauperum*, printed 1465, now in the British Museum, well illustrated in Plate XII of Victor Scholderer, *Johann Gutenberg* (British Museum Publication, 1970).
17. Scholderer 1970, p. 12.
18. Illustrated in Plates VII and VIII of Scholderer.
19. *The Obedience of a Christian Man*, preface.
20. Parker edition, 156–157, echoing the similar complaint of Wyclif, *Opus Evangelicum*, 3.38.
21. Later dean of St Paul's, and founder of St Paul's School.
22. McConica 1991, pp. 28–29, instancing a whole host of familiar phrases stemming from that work: 'a necessary evil', 'to leave no stone unturned', 'the grass is greener over the fence', 'to look a gift horse in the mouth', and many others. The popularity of the work struck me when I looked for it in the Bodleian. The standard modern copy is missing – still popular enough to be stolen – but there are editions published in 1513, 1514, 1517, 1519 (two editions), 1521 (two editions), 1526, 1528, 1532, 1535, etc.
23. Cf. MacCulloch 2003, p. 100.
24. Hall 1809, p. 763.
25. Quoted by MacCulloch 2003, p. 203.

Chapter 5: The King James Bible

1. See Duffy 1992, chs. 11 and 12.
2. *Letters of Henry VIII* (ed. M. St. Clare Byrne; Cassell 1968) 421.
3. Mozley 1953, p. 109.
4. Sic. The 1534 edition of Luther does not, of course, use capitals for nouns.
5. Pollard 1911, p. 196.
6. Fry 1865.
7. The notes of subsequent editions become progressively more Calvinistic and anti-Catholic: the note on Revelation 11:2 applies it directly to the accession of Pope Boniface VIII!
8. Ashton 1969, p. 15.
9. Hill 1993, p. 34.
10. Cited by McGrath 2001, p. 266.
11. Coleridge 1980, vol. 2, pp. 23–31.
12. Cronin 1955, p. 21
13. Satow 1888.
14. Hastings 1990, p. 281.
15. Roe, *History of the British and Foreign Bible Society 1905–1954*, p. 11.

Chapter 6: Modern Versions of the Bible in English

1. An impressively thorough survey of versions before 1980 is given by Lewis 1981. He lists many kinds of data, recognising that every reader will evaluate them according to personal preference.
2. Tolkien 1981, p. 378.
3. A certain qualification is not out of place. Each change proposed from the French 1972 edition had to be agreed with the then director of the Jerusalem School, which was not always forthcoming.
4. Barr 1974, p. 387.
5. These and other features are enthusiastically welcomed by Panning 1973.
6. Ernest P. Frerichs in ABD 6, p. 838.
7. That is, it was not sufficiently close to the verbal shape of the original language.

Chapter 7: The Bible and Vatican II

1. Commentary on Galatians.
2. *On the Babylonian Captivity of the Church*, in Dillenberger 1961, p. 266.
3. MacCulloch 2003, p. 144.
4. MacCulloch 2003, p. 149.
5. Tanner 1990, p. 664.
6. Denzinger 1957, p. 707.
7. In fact it is arguable that they were simply taking seriously the principles of modern biblical scholarship.
8. Related to me by the Principal, R.A.F. MacKenzie, in 1963.
9. Fritz-Leo Lentzen-Deis, SJ.
10. In the same vein, when he came to speak to us students at Jerusalem, he was addressed as 'Your Eminence' (the correct address to a cardinal). 'No, thank you,' he replied amusingly, '"Your Beatitude" [the address to a Patriarch] is quite enough'. Incidentally, nowadays discussion at international meetings in Rome (such as the Biblical Commission) range over the widely-understood modern languages, English, French, German, Italian and Spanish.
11. Harry Y. Gamble in ABD, article on New Testament Canon.
12. Rahner 1961, p. 49.
13. Gospel of Thomas, II.4, in James 1924, p. 49.
14. Eusebius, *Historia Ecclesiastica*, 6.12.
15. It is both interesting and important to note Karl Rahner's position (writing before the council): 'The Two Sources Theory (to coin a phrase) is but a possible interpretation of the Council [of Trent] which is not supported by the unanimous opinion either of the Fathers, or of the medieval theologians. Moreover, it could never claim general consent in the post-Tridentine period, but remained only an opinion.' (*Inspiration in the Bible* [Herder, 1961], p. 36). This suggests that, like so much else at Trent, the Two-Sources approach was a knee-jerk reaction against the Reformers.
16. Butler 1967, p. 38.

17. This is noted by L. Visscher, an observer from the World Council of Churches, in a letter quoted by Hanjo Sauer in Sauer 2003, p. 208: 'The scheme is an expression of this unresolved theological situation. Not only does it open the way to a new discussion of the problem of scripture and tradition, but in addition it is a solemn proof of the fact that uncertainty can exist regarding questions that seemed decided once and for all.'

18. It has been neatly characterized by Robert Murray (in Hastings 1991, p. 76) as 'learned ignorance'.

19. Butler 1967, p. 49.

20. In 1974, a decade after the council, at a conference at Hawkstone Hall, Bishop Butler (as Abbot Christopher Butler had become) said that he considered *Dei Verbum* to be the most important document of Vatican II; it would have the most far-reaching effect on the life of the Church.

21. E.g. *On the Babylonish Captivity of the Church*, the early pages.

22. A superb example of the puzzled distress felt by a loyal son of the Church is provided by the reflections of Père Lagrange on his first visit to Sinai (on camels) in 1893: 'On the other hand, is the Pentateuch the historical account of facts? How was it possible to move the millions of people referred to in the text around, not a limitless desert as flat as a sheet of paper, but those steep waterless valleys? Was it not necessary to conclude that perfectly historical facts had been idealized in order to become symbolic of God's people?' (Lagrange 1985, p. 39).

23. Denzinger 1957, no. 2145–2147.

24. At lunch in the English College, Rome, September 1963.

BIBLIOGRAPHY

Ackroyd, P.R.   *Cambridge History of the Bible*, vol. 1, ed. P.R. Ackroyd and C.F. Evans (Cambridge, CUP, 1970)

Alberigo, G.(ed.)   *History of Vatican II* (Leuwen, Peeters, 2003)

Ashton, R. (ed.)   *James I by his Contemporaries* (London, Hutchinson, 1969)

Augustine   *Nicene and Post-Nicene Fathers*, vol. 1 (Peabody, MA., Hendrickson, 1995)

Barr, J.   'After five years: a retrospect on two major translations of the Bible' (*Heythrop Journal* 15 [1974])

Barton, J. and Muddiman, J. (ed.) *The Oxford Bible Commentary* (Oxford, OUP, 2001)

Brakke, D.   *Athanasius and the Politics of Asceticism* (Oxford, Clarendon Press, 1995)

Brown, R.E. (ed.)   *New Jerome Biblical Commentary* (London, Chapman, 1989)

Bruce-Mitford, R.L.S. *The Art of the Codex Amiatinus* (Jarrow Lecture, 1967)

Butler, C.   *Theology of Vatican II* (London, Darton, Longman and Todd, 1967)

Casey, M.   *Aramaic Sources in Mark's Gospel* (Cambridge, CUP, 1998)

Cassiodorus   *Cassiodori Senatoris Institutiones*, ed. R.A.B. Mynors (Oxford, Clarendon Press, 1937)

Cavallin, H.C.   *Life After Death* (Lund, Gleerup, 1974)

Coleridge, H.J.   *Life and Letters of St Francis Xavier* (London, Burns & Oates 1980)

Colgrave, B. (ed.)   *Paris Psalter* (Copenhagen, Rosenkilde & Bagger, 1958)

Crawford, S.J. (ed.)   *The Old English Version of the Heptateuch* (Oxford, OUP, 1922)

Cronin, V.   *The Wise Man from the West* (London, Hart-Davis, 1955)

Daniell, D.   *The Bible in English* (Yale, Yale UP, 2003)

Deanesly, M .   *The Lollard Bible* (Cambridge, CUP 1920)

Denzinger, H.   *Enchiridion Symbolorum*, ed K. Rahner (Rome, Herder, 1957)

Dillenberger, J. (ed.) *Martin Luther, selections from his writings* (New York, Doubleday, 1961)

Duffy, E.   *The Stripping of the Altars* (Yale, Yale UP, 1992)

Elliott, K. and Moir, I. *Manuscripts and the Text of the New Testament* (Edinburgh, T & T Clark, 1995)

Erasmus   *Complete Works of Erasmus*, tr. R.A.B. Mynors (Toronto, University of Toronto Press)

Field, F.   *Origenis Hexaplorum quae supersunt* (Oxford, OUP, 1875)

Frend, W.H.C.   *The Rise of Christianity* (London, Darton, Longman and Todd, 1984)

Freedman, D.N. (ed.)   *Anchor Bible Dictionary* (New York, Doubleday, 1992), articles:
'Marcion, Gospel of' by R.M. Grant
'Marcion' by J.J. Clabeaux
'New Testament Canon' by H.Y. Gamble
'Thomas, Gospel of' by R. Cameron

Fry, F.   *A Description of the Great Bible 1539* (London, n.pub., 1865)

Hall, E.   *Hall's Chronicle* (London, J. Johnson, 1809)

Hastings, A. (ed.)   *Modern Catholicism* (London, SPCK, 1991)

Hastings, A.   *The Church in Africa, 1450–1950* (Oxford, Clarendon Press, 1990)

Henry VIII   *Letters* (ed. M. St Clare Byrne; London, Cassell, 1968)

Hill, J.   *The English Bible and the Seventeenth Century Revolution* (London, Allen Lane, 1993)

Hurtado, L.   *Lord Jesus Christ* (Grand Rapids, MI., Eerdmans, 2003)

James, M.R.   *The Apocryphal New Testament* (Oxford, Clarendon Press, 1924)

Jeremias, J.   *The Parables of Jesus* (London, SCM Press, 1972)

Johnson, L.T.   *The Real Jesus* (San Francisco, CA., HarperSanFrancisco, 1996)

Kenny, A.   *Wyclif, the morning star of the Reformation* (Oxford, OUP, 1985)

Kinzig, W.   'Καινη. διαθηκη: the title of the New Testament in the second and third centuries', *Journal of Theological Studies* 45 (1994), 519–544

Kloppenborg Verbin, J.S.   *Excavating Q, the history and setting of the Sayings Gospel* (Edinburgh, T &T Clark, 2000)

Lagrange, M.-J.   *Père Lagrange, Personal Reflections and Memoirs* (New York, Paulist Press, 1985)

Lewis, J.P.   *The English Bible from KJV to NIV* (Grand Rapids, MI., Baker Book House, 1981)

Livingstone, E.A. (ed.)   *Oxford Dictionary of the Christian Church* (Oxford, OUP, 1974)

Lüdemann, G.   *Jesus after 2000 Years* (London, SCM Press, 2001)

Lumby, J. (ed.)   *Chronicon* (London, Eyre & Spottiswoode, 1895)

Luther, M.   *Martin Luther, selections from his writings*, ed. J. Dillenberger (New York, Doubleday, 1961)
Luther's Primary Works, ed. H. Wace (London, Hodder & Stoughton, 1896), 'On the Babylonish Captivity', pp. 294–410)

MacCulloch, D.   *Reformation, Europe's House Divided* (Harmondsworth, Penguin, 2003)

McConica, J.   *Erasmus* (Oxford, OUP, 1991)

McGrath, A.   *In the Beginning* (New York, Doubleday, 2001)

Minns, D.   *Irenaeus* (London, Chapman, 1994)
Moule, C.F.D.   *The Making of the New Testament* (London, A & C
                             Black,1962)
Mozley, J.F.   *Coverdale and his Bibles* (Cambridge, Lutterworth
                             Press, 1953)
Mynors, R.A.B. (ed.)   *Cassiodori Senatoris Institutiones* (Oxford, Clarendon
                             Press, 1937)
                             Complete Works of Erasmus (Toronto, University of
                             Toronto Press)
Neuhaus, R.J.   http://www.bible.researcher.com/nab.html
Pagels, E.   *The Gnostic Gospels* (London, Weidenfeld &
                             Nicholson, 1979)
Panning, Armin J.   'The New American Standard Bible – Is this the
                             Answer?' in *Wisconsin Lutheran Quarterly* 70 (1973)
Paris Psalter   ed. B. Colgrave (Copenhagen, Rosenkilde & Bagger,
                             1958)
Pelikan, J.   *The Emergence of the Catholic Tradition 100–600*
                             (Chicago, Chicago UP, 1971)
Pollard, A.   *Records of the English Bible* (Oxford, OUP, 1911)
Rahner, K.   *Inspiration in the Bible* (Freiburg, Herder, 1961)
Raine. J. (ed.)   *Historia Dunelmenses Scriptores Tres* (London, Surtees
                             Society, vol. 9, 1839)
Read-Heimerdinger, J.   *The Bezan Text of Acts: a contribution of discourse
                             analysis to textual criticism* (London, Sheffield
                             Academic Press, 2002)
Robinson, J.A.T.   *Redating the New Testament* (London, SCM Press,
                             1976)
Robinson, J. M.   *The Nag Hammadi Library in English* (Leiden, Brill,
                             1977)
Robinson, J.T.   *The Priority of John* (London, SCM Press, 1985)
Roe, J. M.   *A History of the British and Foreign Bible Society
                             1905–1954* (London, British & Foreign Bible Society,
                             1965)
Sanders, E.P. (ed.)   *Jewish and Christian Self-Definition* (London, SCM
                             Press, 1980)
Satow, E.M.   *The Jesuit Mission Press in Japan, 1591–1610* ([1888]
                             in *Collected Works of Ernest Mason Satow Part 2*, vol.
                             4, Ganesha Publishing, Bristol, 2001)
Sauer, H.   'Doctrinal and Pastoral, the text on Divine Revela-
                             tion' in *History of Vatican II*, ed G. Alberigo, vol. IV
                             (Peeters, Leuwen, 2003)
Scholderer, V.   *Johann Gutenberg* (London, British Museum Publi-
                             cations, 1970)
Smith, M.   *The Secret Gospel* (New York, Harper & Row, 1973)
Sparks, H.D.F.   'Jerome as Biblical Scholar' in *Cambridge History of
                             the Bible*, vol. 1, ed. P.R. Ackroyd and C.F. Evans
                             (Cambridge, CUP, 1970)
Surtees Psalter   *Surtees Society*, London, vols xvi and xix (1845 and
                             1847)
Tanner, N.P.   *Decrees of the Ecumenical Councils* (London, Sheed &
                             Ward, 1990)

Tertullian — *Adversus Marcionem* (Ante-Nicene Fathers, vol. 3, 1885, reprinted Peabody, MA., Hendrickson, 1994)

Tolkien J.R.R. — *Letters*, ed. Humphrey Carpenter (London, Allen & Unwin, 1981)

Vallée, G. — 'Theological and non-theological Motives in Irenaeus' Refutation of the Gnostics' in *Jewish and Christian Self-Definition*, ed. E.P. Sanders (London, SCM, 1980)

Witherington, B. III — *The Jesus Quest* (Exeter, Paternoster Press, 1995)

Wright, N.T. — *The Resurrection of the Son of God* (London, SPCK, 2003)

Wright, T. — *Reliquiae Antiquae* (London, Pickering, 1845)

Wyclif, J. — *De Ecclesia*, ed. J. Loserth (London, The Wyclif Society, 1886)

De Veritate Sacrae Scripturae, ed. R Buddensieg (London, The Wyclif Society, 1905)

INDEX